The Rise of
Brandenburg-Prussia
to 1786

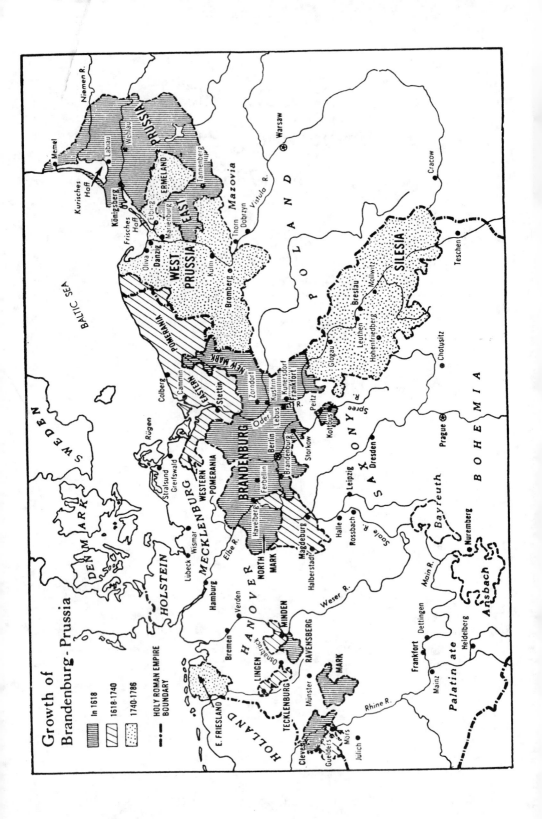

The Rise of

Brandenburg-Prussia

to 1786

REVISED EDITION

by

Sidney B. Fay

Revised by

Klaus Epstein

KRIEGER PUBLISHING COMPANY
MALABAR, FLORIDA

Original Edition 1964
Reprint Edition 1981

Printed and Published by
KRIEGER PUBLISHING COMPANY
KRIEGER DRIVE
MALABAR, FLORIDA 32950

Printed in the United States of America

Library of Congress Cataloging in Publication Data

Fay, Sidney Bradshaw, 1876-
    The rise of Brandenburg-Prussia to 1786.

    Reprint. Originally published: Rev. ed./rev. by Klaus
Epstein. New York : Holt, Rinehart and Winston, 1964.
    Bibliography: p.
    Includes index.
    1. Brandenburg (Germany : Electorate)—History.
I. Epstein, Klaus. II. Title.
DD491.B85F28   1981   943.1′5   81-8334
ISBN 0-89874-377-X   AACR2

10   9   8   7   6   5   4   3

Preface

This little book surveys one of the most extraordinary and surprising stories of modern history: the rise of the territory of Brandenburg—Prussia from an ordinary North German duchy to a great power with an important voice in the diplomatic system of Europe. This achievement owed little to economic forces, for Prussia possessed notoriously sandy soil and was industrially backward until the nineteenth century; it owed nothing to a favorable geographical position, for Prussia lacked natural frontiers and was surrounded by numerous jealous neighbors. Its rise to greatness was rather the result of the successful statecraft of three remarkable rulers of the Hohenzollern dynasty—Frederick William, the Great Elector; Frederick William I; and Frederick the Great—who succeeded in turning their country's liabilities into assets. They believed that Prussia's poverty and precarious position required an exceptional mobilization of all resources—human and economic—to achieve greatness or even guarantee the survival of their state. They built up an army far greater proportionately than appeared warranted by Prussia's small area and population; they centralized administration in their own hands to guarantee adequate resources for their army; they made a bargain with Prussia's landowning aristocracy—the famous Junkers—under which the Junkers served the state in return for ruling their dependent serfs pretty much as they chose; and they provided their subjects with an inspiring example of devoted service to the state irrespective of private happiness. The result of these policies was the development of the phenomenon called "Prussianism": the distinctive spirit of Prussia marked by militarism, absolutism, Junker domination, and selfless devotion to the greatness of the state.

The rise of Prussia is not only of great interest in itself, but assumes additional importance from the subsequent history of Prussia in the nineteenth century. The "Prussian spirit" and the institutions in which it was embodied was to serve as the foundation for the unification of Germany by Bismarck in the 1860s. The Germany of the Second Empire was in many ways an "enlarged Prussia," and was proud of the period of Prussian history described in this volume. It was militarist in the sense of assigning special importance—in resources and prestige—to the army, and repudiating the principle of civilian supremacy. It was absolutist in the sense of affirming monarchical power and repudiating the principle of liberal, parliamentary self-government. It continued to pamper the land-owning Junker aristocracy, and gave its scions preferential treatment in military, diplomatic, and bureaucratic appointments. It made a cult of the duy of serving the state and believed itself far superior to what were called the "decadent, materialistic, and hedonistic Western democracies." The Prussian spirit, whose rise is chronicled in this volume, became, in short, one of the ingredients of the "German problem" of the twentieth century.

The volume here reissued was originally written by Professor Sidney B. Fay in 1937. Professor Fay, though known primarily for his classic work on *The Origin of the World War* (1928), is also the foremost American authority on German history in his generation. He drew deeply from the achievements of the great German historians of the Second Empire—more especially Otto Hintze and Friedrich Meinecke—who were originally his teachers and became his friends. Professor Fay possesses a special gift for presenting their conclusions to an American reading public in a lucid and fair-minded fashion: a difficult task since the very different American historical experience often makes Americans view Prussianism as an incomprehensible and therefore exclusively evil force.

Since Professor Fay's work has stood the test of time, my revisions have been of a minor character. Some detail has been pruned in the early sections, the bibliography has been updated and enlarged with special emphasis upon works in English, and minor changes have been made throughout the book.

K. E.

Brown University,
Providence, R. I.

Contents

The Rise of
Brandenburg-Prussia
to 1786

Hohenzollern Rulers

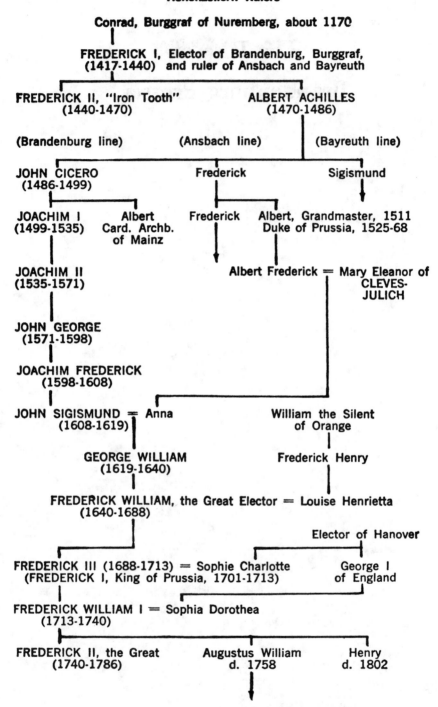

Conrad, Burggraf of Nuremberg, about 1170

FREDERICK I, Elector of Brandenburg, Burggraf,
(1417-1440) and ruler of Ansbach and Bayreuth

FREDERICK II, "Iron Tooth" ALBERT ACHILLES
(1440-1470)   (1470-1486)

(Brandenburg line)   (Ansbach line)   (Bayreuth line)

JOHN CICERO   Frederick   Sigismund
(1486-1499)

JOACHIM I   Albert   Frederick   Albert, Grandmaster, 1511
(1499-1535)   Card. Archb.   Duke of Prussia, 1525-68
               of Mainz

JOACHIM II   Albert Frederick = Mary Eleanor of
(1535-1571)   CLEVES-
                                                 JULICH

JOHN GEORGE
(1571-1598)

JOACHIM FREDERICK
(1598-1608)

JOHN SIGISMUND = Anna   William the Silent
(1608-1619)   of Orange

GEORGE WILLIAM   Frederick Henry
(1619-1640)

FREDERICK WILLIAM, the Great Elector = Louise Henrietta
(1640-1688)

                                        Elector of Hanover

FREDERICK III (1688-1713) = Sophie Charlotte   George I
(FREDERICK I, King of Prussia, 1701-1713)   of England

FREDERICK WILLIAM I = Sophia Dorothea
(1713-1740)

FREDERICK II, the Great   Augustus William   Henry
(1740-1786)   d. 1758   d. 1802

C H A P T E R . . . 1

Gathering
the Lands
(1134–1640)

The North German state of Brandenburg-Prussia, destined to play a great role in European history from King Frederick the Great to Emperor William II, arose from the consolidation of three heterogeneous areas at the beginning of the seventeenth century. The House of Hohenzollern, which had ruled the principality of Brandenburg since 1417, extended its rule over Cleves-Mark in 1614 and East Prussia in 1618 upon the failure of heirs in collateral lines. Of these three territories Brandenburg occupied the center of the north German plain between the Elbe and Oder Rivers; East Prussia the southeastern shore of the Baltic between Lithuania and Poland; while Cleves-Mark was part of the Rhine-Ruhr area in Western Germany.

These three territories were at first united by a personal union only, without a common administration, common army, or uniform political institutions. The objective of successive Hohenzollern princes was to weld

them into a single centralized state and to establish territorial contiguity by annexing the German and Polish
territories that separated Brandenburg from Cleve in the
west and East Prussia in the east. Once this was achieved
the state of Brandenburg-Prussia would dominate northern Germany, split the Holy Roman Empire of which
Austria was the head, and assume an independent role
in the politics of Europe.

The consolidated lands, known as the kingdom of Prussia after the Hohenzollerns secured the royal crown in
1701, showed their European importance by winning a
defensive victory against the combined forces of Austria,
Russia, and France during the Seven Years' War (1756–
1763). Prussia became under Chancellor Bismarck the
nucleus of the new German Empire in 1871 and continued
to play a conspicuous role in German politics until it was
officially dissolved by the Allied Military Government in
1947. The early history of Prussia is necessarily a rather
pedestrian chronicle of parochial events, but interest in it
is enhanced by the knowledge that these events shaped
a monarchy destined for European greatness.

Each of the three original parts of the Prussian realm
was to make its distinctive contribution to the whole.
Brandenburg's chief importance, as was natural enough
from her central geographical position, was that she was
to serve as the core of the Brandenburg-Prussian state.
In Brandenburg were developed the governmental institutions and economic experiments that were gradually
extended over Cleve, East Prussia, and subsequent conquests. Brandenburg was primarily a land of big estates
where land-owning nobles (Junkers) held sway over dependent serfs.

East Prussia, originally the land of the crusading Teutonic Knights, was even more dominated by the Junker
oligarchy than Brandenburg. The influence of this province was enhanced by the prosperity of its ruling class,

a prosperity based upon grain exports to western Europe going through the port and capital city of Königsberg. The Junkers did not, however, confine themselves to running their estates; they also staffed the officer corps and administrative services, both of which became European bywords for efficiency, economy, and integrity.

The Cleves-Mark territories during the period treated in the following pages were made up of quiet meadows with lowing kine and small towns with industries and commerce much inferior to those of the adjacent Dutch. But in the latter part of the nineteenth century this region became blackened with smoking chimneys, noisy with gigantic factories, thronged with steamers and barges, and teaming with population. Through it flows the Ruhr. In it lie the vast coal deposits that have helped transform Germany from an agricultural into an industrial country.

There were also important religious differences between the three territories. In the sixteenth century East Prussia and Brandenburg became and remained predominantly Lutheran, and therefore politically and culturally conservative; but a considerable part of the Cleves population became Reformed (Calvinist) and breathed a more restless and liberal spirit. Its geographical position also brought the Hohenzollerns into contact with the more progressive Dutch and French of western Europe.

What was the early history of these three distinctive lands, and how did they become united?

Beginnings of Brandenburg
(1134–1417)

Charlemagne in his wars of conquest pushed the frontier of the Frankish Empire eastward to the Bohemian Mountains, to the Elbe and Saale rivers, and even a little to the east of the lower Elbe in the Holstein region. Instead of trying to extend his rule over the Slavic tribes beyond this frontier, he was content to establish at various places along it a border count (*Markgraf*) to defend it. One of the most important of these was the North or Old Mark (*Nordmark* or *Altmark*) lying athwart the central Elbe. Trading towns and ecclesiastical foundations gave some opportunity for intercourse between the Teutons to the west and the Slavs to the east of the frontier; but for more than two centuries after Charlemagne's day this line of the Elbe, Saale and Bohemian Mountains continued to form a sharp boundary that ever after distinguished the character of the regions to the west and the east.

In 1134 Albert the Bear was given the rule over the North Mark by the Holy Roman Emperor. He belonged to the Ascanian family, which came originally from the Black Forest region in Southwest Germany. Once in possession of the North Mark, Albert the Bear was ambitious to extend his rule beyond the Elbe. In the course of a long and energetic life (he died in 1170) he conquered the hill-fortress of Brandenburg, baptized and made friends with its Wendish prince, and established a bishopric there. Pushing further, he conquered as far as the Oder and founded bishoprics at Havelberg and Lebus. The native Slav population, known as Wends, was not completely extinguished or driven off. Some of them were Christianized and "left sitting" (*Lassiten*) as the lowest element in the later agricultural population. But the greater part of the Wends disappeared under Albert the Bear and his successors. They were absorbed or replaced by German "colonists" from the west, where the land was insufficient for the growing population. The Ascanians did their utmost to stimulate this colonization movement. As land in Brandenburg was plentiful in amount but poor in quality, peasants from Western Germany were given generously of it—sixty acres to a family instead of the customary thirty-acre holdings in their old homes. Towns

and monasteries were founded. Better agricultural methods and better military organization made it easy for the
incoming German colonists to supersede the old Slavic
natives.

Albert the Bear and his successors were engaged in
almost constant wars with their neighbors, but gradually
added to the North Mark an irregular group of lands that
came to be known as the Mark of Brandenburg. It comprised some 10,000 square miles (roughly the area of the
present State of Vermont).

The Ascanian Margraves of Brandenburg, as a result
of their geographical position, came to be stronger than
any other princes of Germany, with the exception of the
Emperor. In charge of a military outpost against the
enemies of the Empire, they had a relatively large military
feudal force. As they were fighting against the heathen,
they constantly received crusading recruits. The bishoprics
and towns that they founded did not hold their rights
from the Emperor, as in the rest of Germany, but were
directly dependent on the Margraves who kept a strict
control over them.

The Margrave was the sole proprietor of all the conquered land, except so far as he granted it on feudal terms
to his followers and the imported colonists. Though in
the North Mark he was subordinate to the Emperor, in
the lands to the east of the Elbe he enjoyed supreme
judicial as well as military power. So it was natural that,
as early as 1230, the ruler of Brandenburg had come to be
recognized as one of the seven important German princes
who had the right to elect the Emperor. This is indicated in the Saxon Mirror of Justice (*Sachsenspiegel*),
more than a century before the rights and duties of the
Seven Electors were precisely laid down in the constitution of the Empire, known as the Golden Bull of 1356.

When the Brandenburg Ascanians died out in 1320 evil
days came upon the land. Brandenburg passed into the

hands of the Bavarian (Wittelsbach) family, which was engaged in a deadly rivalry with the Hapsburgs for supreme power in the Empire. The Bavarian Electors of Brandenburg cared nothing for the welfare of their new possession. They seldom came in person to rule it. It was merely a land to be heavily taxed and exploited to aid them in their struggle with the Hapsburgs. The situation did not change significantly when the last of the Bavarian Electors, Otto the Lazy, sold the Electorate to the Luxemburg Emperor, Charles IV. The Luxemburgers also neglected their Brandenburg subjects as they became absorbed in their imperial task of fighting the Turks, the Hungarians, and their Hapsburg rivals.

The First Hohenzollerns in Brandenburg (1417–1499)

A new era of prosperity, good government, and princely power began with the arrival of the Hohenzollerns in Brandenburg in the summer of 1412.

The "Zollerns" are first mentioned in a document of 1061. Their ancestral home was a Swabian castle near the sources of the Danube and the Neckar. About 1170 a younger brother, Conrad of Hohenzollern, left the family castle to seek his fortune by the sword and served under Frederick Barbarossa. He was rewarded by being appointed Burggraf of Nuremberg. This made him the Emperor's representative, not in the free imperial city of Nuremberg, but in the central German lands lying about it. As Burggraf he exercised justice, collected fines, checked robbers, and executed the Emperor's decrees. Though the office of Burggraf conferred no land, Conrad and his descendants soon acquired, by marriage, purchase, and conquest, two considerable Franconian territories: the lower land of Ansbach in the valleys of the Regnitz and a branch of the Main to the southwest of Nuremberg, and the higher land of Bayreuth to the northwest of Nuremberg.

Frederick, one of Conrad's descendants two centuries later, by reason of his Franconian possessions and his natural ability, became the close friend and most powerful supporter of the Luxemburg Emperor, Sigismund. He fought for Sigismund against the Turks at the battle of Nicopolis in 1396. He helped him suppress a revolt of Hungarian rebels in 1409 and received as a reward 20,000 florins. He aided in Sigismund's election as Emperor in 1411. In the same year Sigismund inherited Brandenburg, but was too busy with imperial matters to go in person and rule the distant northern Electorate. He therefore appointed his friend Frederick, the Burggraf of Nuremberg and ruler of Ansbach-Bayreuth, as "captain and administrator" of Brandenburg, and in 1417, at the Council of Constance, formally invested him as Elector forever in the lands that he had been ruling for five years.

Frederick I (1417–1440), upon his arrival in Brandenburg in 1412, found a defiant nobility inclined to question his authority, a group of strong towns allied with the Hanseatic League, and a peasantry more or less ruined by the misgovernment of the Bavarian and Luxemburg Electors. It was Frederick's claim to distinction that he changed all this. He broke the power of the recalcitant nobles in vigorous campaigns against their castles. He conciliated the towns. And he began to restore the prosperity of the peasants by protecting them to some extent from the oppression of the Junker landlords. For the first time since the extinction of the Ascanian line of Margraves, the Elector's authority was again strong and respected.

Frederick I, however, did not spend all his time in Brandenburg. After restoring order and authority, he soon left his eldest son, John, to rule in the Electorate, and returned to his favorite Franconian lands and to a

very active part in the affairs of the Empire. He com-
manded the German armies by which Emperor Sigismund
tried to suppress the Hussite revolt. He finally brought
about the negotiations which put an end to the wars with
the Hussites, by granting them tolerant concessions: communion in the form of both bread and wine for the laity,
and free preaching in the national Czechish tongue. He
was a close friend of Enea Sylvio Piccolomini, who sang
his praises; and at the church councils he vigorously supported the papal claims against the conciliar party. He
even had hopes of being elected Emperor at the death of
Sigismund in 1437. But his ambitions were thwarted by
various circumstances and by the jealousy of the other
Electors who preferred to choose a weak Hapsburg, Frederick III (1440–1493), rather than a strong Hohenzollern.

Though Frederick I was best known to his contemporaries as a Franconian prince and imperial statesman, and
never returned to Brandenburg after 1426, he had nevertheless established the Hohenzollerns firmly in the Electorate which was to become the central seat of their
power. In his ability as organizer, commander, and nego-
tiator, he was a worthy forerunner of the Great Elector
and Frederick the Great. Without exaggeration Emperor
Maximilian's tutor could say of him:

This prince was a model of morality and uprightness, such
as is seldom seen in so high a place. By the virtues which
adorned his life and by his zeal for justice, he ennobled himself as a true Elector and made the name of his house famed far
and wide in the whole world. For as the morning star shines
forth in the cloudy mists which surround it, so he shone among
the princes of his time.

Before his death in 1440 Frederick I divided his lands.
He arranged that his eldest son, John, whose nickname,
"the Alchemist," may explain his lack of ability in admin-

istering Brandenburg, should inherit Bayreuth, which was relatively small but prosperous and easy to rule. His second and more vigorous son, Frederick, became Elector of Brandenburg. A third son, Albert, called "Achilles" because of his Herculian strength and his waging of incessant wars, received Ansbach.

Frederick II (1440–1470) dealt a deathblow to the pretensions of the Brandenburg towns, and thereby won for himself the name of "Iron Tooth." The fifteenth century was notable throughout Germany for the efforts of the rising territorial prince (*Landesherr*) to break the power of the medieval towns within his territory. Fortified and self-governing, with wide market and judicial rights, and leagued together, Brandenburg towns formed a kind of state within a state. In their local self-interest they made guild and commercial regulations that oppressed the peasantry and weakened the authority of the Elector. As members of the powerful Hanseatic League they contributed to the support of the Hanseatic navy, sent delegates to the Hanseatic legislative assemblies, and received in return the backing of the League in opposing the Elector.

In 1442 a quarrel broke out in Berlin between the patrician oligarchy and the disfranchised lower classes. Frederick II seized the opportunity to interfere on the side of the latter. He forced the magistrates to surrender to him the keys to the town, the administration of all justice, and a plot of ground near the center of the town on the island formed by the branching of the Spree. Here he built a strong castle and took up his residence. Berlin thus became the political capital of Brandenburg. Living in the midst of its citizens, he was able to quell instantly any revolt, such as one that took place five years later. The little castle which he built was greatly enlarged later, and became the regular residence of the Hohenzollerns. Having thus become master in Berlin, Frederick II easily extended his authority over the other towns of the Electorate. Legislation by the prince in the interests of the whole Electoral territory tended henceforth to supersede the selfish regulations of the local towns.

Frederick II was less fertile in ambitious dynastic projects than his father before him or his brother who succeeded him. But with the aid of able Franconian officials whom he called to his side he proved an efficient and economical administrator. By his patience and prudence he added more lands to Brandenburg than any Elector for the next 200 years. Taking advantage of the financial necessities of the Teutonic Knights in their thirteen years' war with Poland, he bought the area called New Mark from them in 1455. This important territory, half as large as the rest of the Electorate, stretched out to the east of the Oder and was to be an important link in the chain of territories that was to connect Brandenburg and East Prussia.

In addition Frederick II bought from the Emperor the judicial and administrative rights over the Niederlausitz (Lower Lusatia to the southeast of the Electorate) and several small adjacent areas. These gave him a firm foothold in the upper valley of the Spree and good defensive outposts against Polish, Czech, or Hungarian attacks. But in a war with Pomerania he was unsuccessful. Discouraged, and by nature pious and melancholy, he resigned the Electorate in 1470 into the hands of his brother, Albert Achilles, and retired to a castle in Franconia where he died the next year.

Albert Achilles (1470–1486) was already fifty-six years old when he inherited Brandenburg and thus united under one rule, but for the last time, the Electoral and Franconian lands. He was still, however, a man of extraordinary physical vigor and restless ambitions. In his youth he had won prizes at jousting tournaments, and had made a pilgrimage to Jerusalem—more for adventure than piety. He planned many clever schemes that gained for him the dubious title of "the German fox," but which brought him no tangible advantages.

In 1470 Albert drew up for his Franconian lands a very interesting house ordinance (*Hofordnung*). With its detailed account of his officials, with their functions and revenues and the policies to be followed, it gives an excellent picture of the German system of government that was beginning to develop from medieval patriarchal forms into the princely absolutisms of the sixteenth and seventeenth centuries.

Albert also perceived the disastrously weakening effect of the German practice of subdividing principalities among many sons. He therefore issued in 1473 his famous constitution *(Constitutio Achillea)* regulating the succession of the Hohenzollern lands. The Electorate of Brandenburg was now recognized for the first time as the most important part of the Hohenzollern inheritance; it was to go to the eldest son. If there were two other sons, they were to receive Ansbach and Bayreuth. If there were more than three sons, the younger ones were to become ecclesiastics and be provided with small sums of money until bishoprics could be found for them. Thus there would be henceforth at most three ruling lines of Hohenzollern Margraves, and if any of the lines died out its lands were to be united again under the rule of the Electoral branch. In accordance with this wise constitution, Albert's three sons took their respective parts at his death in 1486: John became Elector of Brandenburg; Frederick established a separate line in Ansbach, and Sigismund one in Bayreuth.

Albert, like his two predecessors, was buried in Franconia, where he had passed most of his life. But he was the last Elector to be laid to rest there. Henceforth the Electors lived, died, and were buried in Brandenburg, which they had at last come to regard as their real home and chief possession.

John "Cicero" (1486–1499) was really no Cicero.[1] He had no knowledge of refined Latin, and, like most of his Brandenburg subjects, was innocent of any interest in the new Renaissance movement that was beginning to transform the intellectual life of South Germany. His reign opened a century of comparative peace in Brandenburg, in which the chief interest lies in the internal development of the Electorate.

Joachim I (1499–1535): The Roman Law and the Lutheran Movement

Joachim I was only fifteen years of age at the death of his father in 1499. According to the Golden Bull he could not rule as Elector until he became eighteen. However, he promptly rejected the proffered regency of his Franconian uncle, Frederick, and appeared in person as a full-fledged Elector at the Diet of Augsburg in 1500. He had high ideas of his powers as a prince and was determined to show his people that he intended to be master. In two years he had forty robber-nobles decapitated or hanged. By a strict police ordinance of 1515 he placed the maintenance of order in the towns directly under the strict surveillance of his central government and reorganized the urban police. Though hardly a shining example of morality in his own personal life—he kept many mistresses—he made genuine efforts to raise the clergy from their ignorance and immorality.

His most important contribution to his country was the foundation in 1506 of the first university in the Electorate, at Frankfort on the Oder. Though intensely con-

[1] The inappropriate name Cicero which has stuck to John was not known to his contemporaries; it was first invented by a pious chronicler eighty years after his death.

servative and little imbued with the spirit of the "new learning," the university was soon a flourishing institution; it even drew students from other parts of Germany, as may be seen from the matriculation lists that have been published. Under Joachim I it remained a bulwark of Roman Catholicism against the rising tide of Lutheranism. It even conferred a degree upon Tetzel, the famous indulgence seller, after he had expounded his views on papal infallibility within its walls. Its most important influence was in the training of students of Roman law. These jurists, like the *légistes* in medieval France, formed a body of able administrators and shrewd councilors ready to serve the prince in his efforts further to break the power of the nobles, clergy, and towns, and make himself absolute ruler. Preferring the precise, written, and highly developed Roman law in which they had been trained and took pride, to the indefinite, customary German law, which was largely handed down by word of mouth and varied greatly from locality to locality, these university-trained jurists tended to apply Roman instead of German legal principles. They contributed to that extraordinary phenomenon, known as "the reception of the Roman law," by which a foreign system of jurisprudence was imposed almost imperceptibly upon Germany. This phenomenon was not peculiar to Brandenburg. It was taking place throughout the Holy Roman Empire in the course of the sixteenth century. A great impetus had been given to it by Emperor Maximilian's decree of 1495 that at least eight of the sixteen judges of the Supreme Court of the Empire *(Reichskammergericht)* must be learned in Roman law.

Though Joachim I added no territory directly to Brandenburg in his own day, his relatives secured appointments that later greatly increased the Hohenzollern possessions. His cousin Albert was elected Grandmaster of the Teutonic Order in 1511. The Reformation, breaking

out soon thereafter, provided him with the opportunity
to transform the territory of the Order into a hereditary
duchy for himself and his heirs; in 1618 this was inherited
by the Electors of Brandenburg, as we shall see later on.
Joachim's brother, Albert, when only twenty-four years
of age, was elected Bishop of Halberstadt and Archbishop
of Magdeburg in 1513. The following year he became
Archbishop of Mainz, thus giving the Hohenzollerns two
of the seven seats in the Electoral College of the Empire
during the critical Reformation years. Family influence
and imperial favor combined to secure the election of
Hohenzollern younger sons in Halberstadt and Magdeburg for a century and a half thereafter (with a single
exception), until the rich and extensive sees were finally
incorporated into the Brandenburg-Prussian state under
the Great Elector in 1648 and 1680 respectively.

Joachim I was one of the most determined opponents
of the new Lutheran doctrines that were spreading like
wildfire in Germany. He took a strong stand against the
Wittenberg monk at the famous Diet of 1521, and tried
to enforce the Edict of Worms in Brandenburg by threatening the direst penalties to any of his subjects who dis-
obeyed it. He conceived a bitter personal hatred for
Luther and believed his subversive teachings to be directly
responsible for the great Peasant Revolt of 1525. His chief
aim in his later years was to check Lutheranism. In order
to create for his son, Joachim, a bond that should hold
him firm to the Catholic faith, he chose for him a Catholic
wife, Magdalene, daughter of Duke George of Saxony.
Duke George had presided at the Disputation of Leipzig,
and cried out, at Luther's admission that the Hussite
opinions were not all wrong: "God help us, the pestilence!" But all Joachim's efforts could not prevent the
spread of the Lutheran doctrines among the people of
the Electorate. Even in the bosom of his own family the
heresy made its appearance. His own wife, Elizabeth,

daughter of the King of Denmark, turned Lutheran in 1527. Her husband's threats so frightened her that she fled at night from Berlin, and sought refuge for eighteen years with Luther's friend, John the Steadfast of Saxony. Meanwhile Joachim's Franconian cousins, as well as Albert, Duke of Prussia, had become champions of the Protestant party. Even his brother, the Cardinal-Archbishop of Mainz, was suspected of wavering.

Joachim II (1535–1571): New Political Institutions

Joachim II, upon the death of his father, was at once besieged by both religious parties to join their side. Melanchthon made several visits to Berlin and revived that early inclination toward Lutheran teachings that Joachim II had undoubtedly felt nearly twenty years before after a personal talk with Luther. Delegations from his own towns and nobles came to beg him to adopt Lutheran forms. On the other hand, the papal nuncios and the Emperor sought to keep him firm in the old faith by making concessions of various kinds. For four years Joachim II hesitated, replying in noncommittal language that in the matter of the Christian religion and ceremonies he would still continue so to act as to satisfy his conscience, his honor, and his responsibility to Almighty God and the Emperor.

By 1539, however, his subjects became more clamorous. Even the Bishop of Brandenburg openly adopted Lutheran practices. A delegation of Berlin burghers petitioned that at the Easter Communion they be allowed to receive both the bread and the wine as Luther taught. Joachim's most trusted councilors advised him that the time was ripe for the introduction of the Reformation in Brandenburg. Accordingly, on November 1, 1539, Joachim finally received the communion in both kinds. The momentous step took place in the new cathedral just built at Berlin with much expense, which he adorned with relics gathered from monasteries all over the Electorate, and sanctified with the bones of his ancestors which he transferred from the family vault in the cloister at Lehnin.

Joachim II, however, did not intend that his adoption of the Reformation should lead to a political rupture with the Emperor or the Catholic princes. To his Catholic father-in-law he took pains to explain: "We have no intention of subjecting ourselves wholly to the Lutheran teaching or of introducing any innovations. We simply wish to secure uniformity of ceremonial and discipline in our lands and thereby put an end to the *disputationes* and *quaestiones* by which the common man is nowadays stirred up." He allowed his wife to remain Roman Catholic and have her priests with her. He did not join the Protestant Schmalkald League or take part in the religious wars in Germany. He remained in close political touch with the Emperor throughout his life, endeavoring always to find a peaceful basis of settlement between Lutherans and Catholics, such as was finally achieved in the Peace of Augsburg in 1555. He pursued a middle-of-the-road policy, keeping a foot in each of the religious camps, and sparing his people the sufferings of a religious war.

Joachim II's adoption of Lutheranism gave him increased powers and duties. The princely absolutism that his father had sought to establish seemed at first about to take another step forward. According to Luther's Erastian principles, the ruling prince took the place of the Pope and became supreme head of the church in each of the German territories that adopted Lutheranism. So Joachim II, as *summus episcopus* in Brandenburg, issued in 1540 a long eccleciastical ordinance, a part of which, as he proudly said, "I wrote with my own hand." It reflected his desire to stand well with both religious parties. While it emphasized some of Luther's fundamental doctrines, such as justification by faith, the marriage of the clergy, and communion with the wine and the bread, it retained as much as possible of the old Roman ceremonial: the elevation of the Host, Latin chants, genuflexions before the crucifix, and Extreme Unction. It provided Brandenburg with a confession of faith, a catechism, and a book of eccleciastical discipline and ceremonial. Every one had to obey the new ordinance: "If any one should be so obstinate as to refuse to conform to this very Christian regulation, we shall permit him, by our generosity, to go and reside in some other land where he can live as he chooses." This half-tolerant principle, that the prince was to determine the religion of his territory, but that those of his subjects who differed from him might emigrate, was in accordance with the famous maxim, *Cujus regio, ejus religio,* which was finally legalized in the Empire for Catholic and Lutheran princes in 1555 and for Calvinists in 1648.

Organization of the Lutheran Church and Consistorium

By his ecclesiastical ordinance Joachim II succeeded in winning hearty letters of congratulation from Luther and Melanchthon, and at the same time received from the Emperor a formal approval of it, at least until a general or national church council should regulate definitely all religious differences in Germany. But Joachim did not intend that his church should be bound to either of the religious parties or involved in their wars. He regarded himself as independent: "I do not want to be bound any more to Wittenberg than to Rome; I do not say, *Credo sanctam Romanam* or *Wittenbergensem,* but *catholicam ecclesiam,* and my church at Berlin is just as much a true Christian church as that at Wittenberg."

Joachim also sent out commissioners who made a careful visitation of every parish, taking an inventory of church property, transferring superfluous silver vessels to Berlin, and making proper provision for the support of local pastors and sextons. Like his contemporary Henry VIII of England, he dissolved most of the monasteries and nunneries and some other pious foundations. He placed the administration of the three bishoprics (Brandenburg, Havelberg, and Lebus) in the hands of his relatives. This secularization of church lands meant the virtual disappearance of the clergy as one of the three political Estates of the land. Henceforth, the Diet instead of consisting of three estates, as formerly was composed of only two, the nobility and the towns. The revenues from the church lands ought to have strengthened the Elector financially. But they did so only to a small extent. In many cases the revenues were turned over to local uses, especially to the support of schools, hospitals, and the local ministers. Like Henry VIII, Joachim II gave away a large part of the secularized ecclesiastical lands to nobles and officials; most of the remainder he soon burdened with heavy mortgages in return for cash loans. It made little difference that he had been warned by the Diet not to do this and had promised that he would not do so. Within a dozen years after his adoption of the Reformation, he had lost the revenues from so many secularized lands that the nobles and towns had to take steps to help him redeem the mortgaged property, and so recover revenues that he need never have lost if he had been a more economical business administrator.

In 1543 Joachim II completed his reorganization of the church in Brandenburg by the appointment of a permanent Eccleciastical Commission (Consistorium) to assist him in appointing pastors and superintendents, hearing ecclesiastical cases, and administering the rest of the church business that had formerly been in the hands of the three bishops. This consistorium, composed of an ecclesiastical superintendent, a Roman-trained lawyer, and two or three other officials, with clerks, a seal of its own, and a regular time and place of meeting, was one of the first governing boards that differentiated itself from the rest of the household administration and began a separate institutional existence with specialized functions of its own.

Treasury, Supreme Court, and Privy Council

In the middle of the sixteenth century two great constitutional changes were taking place in Brandenburg. The first was the beginning of the separation from the Elector's household of new organs of central government through the division of labor of the Elector's Council (*Rat*) into three bodies having charge respectively of legal, financial, and general political business. An exactly analogous development had taken place three centuries earlier in France and England with the threefold branching forth of the *curia regis*—this time lag of three centuries reveals dramatically the comparative "backwardness" of Germany in the sixteenth century. The second change was the sudden decline of the Elector's authority and the rise to political power of the privileged nobles and towns represented in the Estates (*Landstände*)—a situation that lasted for a century, until the Great Elector crushed the Estates and established his own absolute power.

In Brandenburg before Joachim II's reign, as in the other principalities in Germany, there had been a very close organic connection between the management of the prince's domestic household and the administration of the territory over which he ruled. No clear distinction had existed between the prince in his private capacity as patrimonial feudal owner of large landed estates with an extensive domestic establishment and the sovereign in his public capacity as the political ruler of the territorial state. The personal interests and affairs of the prince were still inextricably associated and interwoven with those of the state. The idea of public revenues, as distinct from the ruler's personal private income, had scarcely emerged. The government of the territory was still for the most part carried on by the prince's domestic household officials, most of whom actually still lived in the castle with him. They ate in the same dining room with him; at night they received candles from the same silver closet, and wine and beer from the same cellar; and they stabled their horses in the same stable with his. The very title borne by some of the most important political officials—Marshal, Chamberlain, Master of the Household, Manager of the Storehouse—were reminiscent of their originally domestic character. They drew no distinction between the domestic service of the household and the public service of the state, for the Elector's household was thought of as coextensive with the Electorate. The Marshal, for instance, after a busy morning going the rounds of the stable, inspecting the saddles or horseshoeing, would join the Elector's other councilors, and discuss in council high matters of state policy, or perhaps receive and negotiate with foreign ambassadors. But every evening he would descend to the humbler but necessary task of noting how many people had dined that day at the Elector's tables, how much food was on hand for the morrow, and what necessaries ought to be ordered. From the inspection of the kitchen or the reprimanding of a disorderly scullion, he might go straight forth to lead the Elector's army against the enemy or to negotiate a treaty in a foreign capital.

By the time of the reign of Joachim II, however, came the glimmering consciousness of the distinction between the private and public aspects of the ruler. As the Elector gathered more lands, played a more prominent part in German politics, and secularized the church lands, the business of the household was increasing enormously in volume, becoming more complicated, and needing to be sorted out and dealt with by specially trained officials. These were furnished more and more by the university students trained in the newly introduced Roman law. They tended to displace the old nobles who were bored with details and with a legal terminology that they did not very well understand. To meet this need of specialization of function and division of labor, the Elector began to assign special councilors or other officials to handle special matters. Joachim II, as we have already seen, handed over ecclesiastical affairs to the Consistorium in 1543. The three remaining main branches of business—financial, judicial, and political—were gradually given over respectively to the Treasury, the Supreme Court and (after 1604) to the Privy Council, as indicated in the table at the end of this book.

1. The Treasury (*Kammer,* that is the "chamber," where the Elector's hoard was originally kept) consisted of three bureaus. (a) The Comptroller's Office (*Amtskammer*) had general charge of the administration of the Elector's domain lands. These provided his main revenues, both in the form of rents in cash, but principally in the form of grain, meat, beer, firewood, and other produce in kind, which were either consumed in the district (*Amt*) where they were produced or hauled to the storehouse in Berlin for the support of the Elector and his household. (b) The Exchequer (*Hofrentei*) at Berlin received the cash revenues from tolls, beer taxes, millstone and other monopolies, and also the surplus cash revenues flowing from the

sale of produce from the domains; from these revenues it paid out the cash expenditures of the Elector's household. The Treasury proper (*Kammer*), later known as (c) the Privy Purse (*Chatulle*), received the surplus turned over by the Exchequer above the running expenses of the government, and also various revenues from other sources.

2. The Supreme Court (*Kammergericht*) was first organized under Joachim II around 1540. It sat in the Elector's council chamber at Berlin on Mondays, Wednesdays, and Fridays so that some of the judges might be free to sit with the Consistorium that met on Tuesdays and Thursdays. It served as the highest court of appeal from the lower courts in Brandenburg, and no appeal could be taken from it to the Imperial Court, because the seven Electors, according to the Golden Bull, enjoyed the *Privilegio de non appellando*.

3. The Council (*Rat*) dealt with all the remaining political and administrative business, and especially with questions of foreign policy. It was presided over by the Elector himself or by his chancellor, and was not at first sharply differentiated from the Supreme Court; some of the same men sat in both bodies, and the Elector reserved some lawsuits for decision in his Council. But in 1604 the Elector, Joachim Frederick, was faced with difficult questions of foreign policy: especially negotiations by which he hoped to make good eventually his claims to East Prussia, Cleves-Mark, and other territories. He felt that he needed the advice of men with more experience and a wider point of view than the narrow-visioned Brandenburgers in his Council. He therefore appointed to it a Franconian, a Saxon, and a Rhineland Calvinist who had been prominent in Cleves-Mark. The old Council, thus enlarged, was given precise rules and an organization of its own, and was henceforth known as the Privy Council (*Geheimer Rat*).

Development of the Principal Organs of Government in Brandenburg-Prussia

Dotted lines ––––––– Organs of Brandenburg Electorate   Solid lines –––––– General Organs of Prussian State

1500   1600 1619   1640   1688   1713   1740   1786

George William | Frederick William, the Great Elector | Frederick III, (I as King) | Frederick William I | Frederick the Great

War or District Commissars   1655 General Commissariat
Kriegs-Marsch- or Kreiskommissars   *Generalkommissariat*

1686 Navy Chest
Marine- or Chargenkasse
1682 Stamp-tax Chest
Stempelkasse
1680 Commerce Board
Commerzkollegium
1674 Field War Chest   General War Chest
Feldkriegskasse   *Generalkriegskasse*

1722 Recruiting Chest
Rekrutenkasse

Bushel and Tolls Chest
Metz-Lizentkasse War Chest
Kriegskasse
Land-tax Chest
Kontributionskasse
1668 General Staff
Generalstab
Sparr

1630-1641
War Council
Kriegsrat

Immediate Commissions

General Directory: 4, later 9, Depts.
General-Ober-Finanz-Kriegs-und Domainen-Directorium

King's Chest
Dispositionskasse

King in his Cabinet

1698 State Conference for Foreign Affairs
Staatskonferenz or Cabinetsministerium

1703 High Court of Appeal
Oberappellationsgericht

1713 General Finance Directory
General-Finanz-Directorium

1658 Judicial Committee of the Privy Council
Justizrat

1689 Privy Comptroller's Office
Geheime Hofkammer

1713 General Finance Chest
General-Finanz-Kasse or Domainenkasse

1713 Brandenburg Exchequer
Landrentei

1651 State Finance Councillors
Staatskammerraets

1673 Court State Chest
Hofstaatskasse

Postal Chest
Postkasse

Council   Privy Council
Rat   Geheime Rat

Administration and Foreign Affairs

Elector in his Feudal Council

Ecclesiastical

Financial

Judicial

Comptroller's Office
Amtskammer

Privy Purse
Chatulle

Exchequer
Hofrentei

Treasury (*Kammer*)

1543 Consistory
Konsistorium

1540 Supreme Court
Kammergericht

Dual Government of the Elector and the Estates

This budding off of new organs of government with specialized functions of their own at first sight suggests that Joachim II was moving further in the direction of efficiency in administration and the establishment of absolutism. But his reckless extravagance actually brought about a development in precisely the opposite direction, transferring much of the power from the prince to the Estates and establishing for a century the divided and weak system of government known as "dualism."

Until the time of Joachim II the Brandenburg Electors had been mostly good managers and economical rulers. They had been able to live within their regular income from their domains and their regalian revenues, with occasional taxes granted by the Estates. But Joachim II was recklessly extravagant. He gave away money and lands to his favorite friends and mistresses, squandered his substance on costly buildings, sumptuous feasts, hunting parties, tournaments, and imposing liveries. No less than 452 horses formed the train with which he appeared to take part in an election of the Emperor. At the same time he had to pay his share of the troops for the defense of the Empire against the Turks and to protect his lands during the Schmalkald Wars, in which, however, he took no part. To meet his expenses he borrowed money from the Jews and others at usurious rates, and began to mortgage his domains. As a result, within five years he found himself so hopelessly in debt that he had to appeal to the Estates for help.

Accordingly, in 1540 the Estates, representing the nobles and towns of the Electorate, generously came to his assistance, but only at the price of important political concessions on his part. The Estates assumed responsibility for the debts to the extent of 850,000 talers, an enormous sum for those days.[2] In return the Elector promised "to undertake no weighty matter, touching the weal or woe of the land, except with the previous advice and consent of the Estates." He promised them a share in the government such as they had never before aspired to. He consented that the management of the debts that they assumed should be taken out of his own hands and placed under a committee representing the Estates. He also promised to contract no new debts and to mortgage no more of his domains.

Joachim II, however, had not learned the lesson that this should have taught him. He was too much of a spendthrift to keep his promise not to borrow further. Usurious interest charges ate up the revenues that were diminished as more domains were mortgaged. In 1550 he had to appeal to the Estates again, and they agreed to take over debts amounting to 1,250,000 talers, again exacting concessions in return. The same thing happened in 1565, when, after long haggling, they became responsible for 1,500,000 more. In spite of this assistance, when the old man died six years later, the Estates found that he still had debts amounting to 2,500,000 talers.

To raise money toward paying off the debts, the Estates agreed to levy taxes, the towns contributing a beer tax and the nobles a land tax. But the Elector had to concede that the collection, administration, and expenditure of these taxes should be exclusively in the hands of the Estates. Thus, by the side of the Elector's Treasury and fiscal agents there rose up a duplicate financial machinery

[2] The taler of the sixteenth century was about the size of the United States silver dollar, which weighs 26.7 grams and is nine-tenths pure silver, but it had at least twenty times the purchasing power of the present American dollar. See F. von Schrötter, *Das preussische Münzwesen* (6 vols., Berlin, 1904–1911), and for tables of prices and values, G. Wiebe, *Zur Geschichte der Preisrevolution des XVI. und XVII. Jahrhunderts* (Berlin, 1895).

(*Ständisches Kreditwerk*), with its own treasure chests, accounting and disbursing officials, and debt obligations, all managed by agents appointed by the Estates and totally independent of the Elector. Some of this machinery lasted until 1821, when the last obligations were discharged. This meant a confusing and disastrous dualism in finance, which extended more or less throughout the government. The Estates eventually had their own troops, separate from those of the Elector; they even tried to pursue a foreign policy at variance with his. And they demanded a share in the appointment of the Elector's officials. This division of control and duplication of machinery deprived the Elector of effective power in domestic legislation and foreign policy, and made Prussian policy especially vulnerable to foreign intrigue and even corruption.

The Brandenburg Estates never secured a positive right of legislation. They could only act as a negative force checking the action of the Elector. On each occasion when he and his successors asked for money, they brought forward long lists of "grievances" that they insisted on having redressed. From a social and economic point of view this was unfortunate, because what they demanded as "redress of grievances" was usually the confirmation of medieval selfish privileges or the granting of new rights at the expense of the peasantry in the country and the lower disfranchised classes in the towns. The peasantry thus became depressed into a condition of servitude. Instead of being able to commute their labor services into money payments and so secure some of the advantages of the general rise in prices in the sixteenth century, like the copyholders in England, they were forced to continue their heavy labor-services for the Junker landlords. Instead of securing protection in the Elector's courts, such as Joachim would have been glad to give them, they were left under the arbitrary jurisdiction of the oppressive nobles. The Elector's efforts to substitute more uniform weights and measures for the great variety of medieval local practices met with persistent obstruction. Almost nothing was done for education, especially after the antagonism between the Elector and the Estates was sharpened by the Elector's adopting for himself in 1613 the Calvinist "Reformed" creed while his subjects continued to adhere to a rigidly narrow Lutheranism. That the selfish interests of the Estates did not triumph more completely at the expense of the Elector and the lower classes was due only to the fact that the social and economic interests of the nobles and towns were often so opposed to one another that they were unable to make a united stand in their demands for redress of grievances.

This dualism of government between the Elector and the Estates, which began with Joachim II, lasted with little change for a century, until the Great Elector. He broke the power of the Estates, established the absolute authority of the Prince, and began the progressive economic and social legislation and the vigorous foreign policy that were to transform the weak Electorate into the strong Brandenburg-Prussian state. Compared with the first Hohenzollerns in Brandenburg, Joachim's immediate successors, John George (1571–1598), Joachim Frederick (1598–1608), and John Sigismund (1608–1619), contributed relatively little that was new in the evolution of the country. Instead, therefore, of tracing their history, it is more important to see how the two other lands, Prussia and Cleves-Mark, were gathered under their rule.

The Teutonic Knights in Prussia to 1525

The geography of Prussia somewhat resembles that of Brandenburg—sandy plains, lakes and sluggish watercourses, an inhospitable soil, and open frontiers. It differs from Brandenburg in having a long seacoast from the Vistula to the Niemen, with two great lagoons almost shut off from the Baltic by long narrow sandspits. The German colonization of Prussia also resembled that of Brandenburg, except that it began a century later, and was carried on by a military-monastic organization instead of by energetic secular princes like Albert the Bear.

The native population, the *Borussi,* or Prussians, belonged to a group sometimes known as the Letto-Lithuanian, or Baltic, group. They spoke a language that stands philologically between the Teuton and the Slav languages. From the fourth to the thirteenth centuries the Prussians had lived a harmless amphibious existence between the sand and the sea, following their heathen rites and occasionally selling amber to the peoples of the west. A few bold missionaries had sought to make converts among them, but had suffered martyrdom for their pains. With the Poles to the south and the west they had frequent border conflicts, until finally, in 1226, a Polish prince Conrad of Mazovia, unable to conquer or Christianize them, called to his aid the Teutonic Order.

This famous organization arose during the Third Crusade, when certain merchants of Bremen and Lübeck spread the sails of their ships as tents in the Holy Land to afford a shelter and hospital to their crusading brethren. Like the Knights Templar and Hospitalers, which were organized a few years earlier, the Teutonic Knights soon came to form a powerful military-monastic crusading Order. But they were at a disadvantage as compared with Templars and the Hospitalers. Arising later, they acquired less power in the Holy Land; and being mainly German, they received fewer pious gifts of land than the two other orders which were richly endowed all over western Europe. The Teutonic Knights therefore were glad to accept the call of Conrad of Mazovia for a crusade against the heathen Prussians, especially as they were promised full sovereignty, independent of the Holy Roman Empire, over all lands that they might conquer.

Transferring their forces from the Holy Land and from Venice to Northern Germany, the Teutonic Knights sailed down the Vistula, establishing blockhouses at Thorn, Culm, Elbing, and Marienwerder. Within a quarter of a century they pushed through the sands and forests eastwards, and in 1255 founded Königsberg, named in honor of King Ottokar of Bohemia who assisted in the conquest. In spite of a violent revolt of the native Prussians, which broke out in 1261 and lasted twenty years, the Teutonic Knights gradually made themselves masters of much of the eastern shore of the Baltic from the Vistula to the Gulf of Finland. In 1309 they moved their headquarters from Venice to Marienburg on the Nogat, an eastern outlet of the Vistula. Here they built a magnificent castle, with dormitories, banqueting hall, armory, stables, and a chapel with a mosaic of the Virgin eighteen feet high.

The hundred years from 1309 to 1409 were the golden age of the Teutonic Knights. Young nobles from all over Europe found no greater honor than to come out and fight under their banner and be knighted by their Grandmaster. After conquering the Prussians, they continued crusading against the heathen Lithuanians and against the Russians, as Chaucer indicates in his description of "the parfit gentil knight":

> Ful ofte tyme he hadde the bord bigonne
> Aboven all naciouns in Pruce.
> In Lettow hadde he reysed and in Ruce.

German peasants were settled on the conquered land on the same generous terms as in Brandenburg. Towns were founded and given wide privileges of self-government; they soon joined the Hanseatic League and developed a flourishing trade on the Baltic. The Knights themselves grew rich and prosperous. In 1310 they conquered from the Poles Pomerelia in the valley of the Vistula, and in 1402 purchased the New Mark from the Luxemburg family, thus making a solid avenue of German territory connecting East Prussia with the Holy Roman Empire.

But even in the later years of the golden age the Order was being weakened by tendencies that were ultimately to cause its complete decay and dissolution. It always remained a narrow oligarchy of not more than four hundred Knights. The Order never called into its membership any of its subjects in Prussia, whom it treated with disdain, but recruited itself from noble families in Germany. There was nothing in Prussia to bridge the gulf between the rulers and the ruled.

This gulf between the Knights and their German colonists was increased by the selfish monopolistic commercial policy of the Order. It reserved exclusively to itself the profitable amber trade. It fixed tariff laws that benefited its own export of grain and other produce in competition with the trade of the Prussian country nobles and towns. So the Order came to be generally hated by the Prussian nobles, who looked enviously across the border at the great power and privileges enjoyed by the Polish nobility and by the Prussian towns, which wanted to draw closer their affiliations with the powerful Hanseatic League. This feeling of antagonism gave currency to the rumors that the Knights had become degenerate; that they cared more for eating and drinking than for spreading the gospel among the heathen; that they had more ledgers than prayer books; that at their rich and riotous banquets, instead of observing their original rule of silence at meals, their talk was of horses, women, and unseemly stories. There was undoubtedly much truth in these rumors. Wealth and prosperity, as in the case of the Templars in France, had resulted in moral degeneracy among the Knights themselves and in envy and hatred among the people about them.

Joined to these internal causes of weakness were two external events that further undermined their power. In 1386 Prince Jagello of Lithuania married the Roman Catholic heiress to the Polish throne, became a Christian, and immediately converted all his Lithuanian people. As the Prussians had long since all been conquered and Christianized, and as there could now be no more crusades against the Lithuanians, the Teutonic Knights had no more heathen to proselytize by the sword. They had lost their main reason for existence.

Furthermore, Jagello's marriage united Lithuanian and Poland in a personal union, joining together in a powerful state two neighbors of the Teutonic Order who had hitherto weakened each other by continual wars. The Poles now began to regret having aided in the establishment of a German state along the Baltic that cut them off from the sea. Border conflicts between the Knights and the Poles became frequent. Finally in 1409 Poland declared war on the hated Knights—and was assisted by the Order's own discontented subjects.

The war with Poland marks the beginning of a century of decline and decay in the Teutonic Order, which ended with its complete dissolution in 1525. The Poles gathered a motley army—Poles, Lithuanians, Czechs, Ruthenians, and even some Russians—and advanced against Prussia with a force of perhaps 35,000 all told. Some of the wiser Knights, seeing their own weakness and the chasm of discontent that separated them from their own subjects, advised negotiations. But the majority, self-confident and feverish for battle, insisted on taking up the fight. Collecting their own forces and raising a feudal militia from the nobles and towns in Prussia, they hurried in the heat of July 1410 to meet the Poles at Tannenberg. Though outnumbered nearly two to one, they started to attack. In the

midst of the battle some of their treacherous militia
lowered their standards and left the field. The Knights
fought on with desperate bravery, but were cut down and
killed, or forced to surrender. The flower of the Order
perished. What was worse, their prestige was gone and
the antagonism between them and their own subjects had
been revealed. As a result of their defeat at Tannenberg
they were forced by the First Peace of Thorn in 1411 to
cede Samogitia and Dobrzyn to Poland and to pay the
enormous sum of 4,500,000 marks of silver as a ransom for
the captured Knights.

In the following years two Grandmasters tried to intro-
duce reforms, by restoring the old discipline and by conciliating the nobles and towns in Prussia by giving them
some share in the government. But these Grandmasters
were opposed by the Knights themselves and deposed as
traitors. Nothing shows more sharply the degeneracy and
shortsighted folly of the Order in the fifteenth century
than this refusal to eradicate the weaknesses that had been
partly responsible for the Tannenberg disaster. On the
contrary, the Knights increased the taxes to pay the ransom to Poland and to hire mercenary troops to defend
their waning power, and thereby increased further the
discontent among their subjects.

The Prussian nobles and towns finally formed a league
in defiance of the Order, and in 1453 appealed for help
the King of Poland. The Poles were only too ready to
aid the rebels. So began the terrible Thirteen Years' War,
in which Prussia was ravaged and the Knights utterly defeated. In 1466, by the Second Peace of Thorn, the
Knights had to cede back to Poland the Vistula region
known as Pomerelia or West Prussia, thus giving to Poland again a free outlet to the sea and cutting off East
Prussia from direct contact with Germany. West Prussia
was to remain Polish until Frederick the Great took it
back by the First Partition of Poland in 1772. The Order

was allowed to retain East Prussia (except the wedge-shaped Bishopric of Ermeland that was joined to a Polish Archbishopric), but only as a fief of Poland. Henceforth every new Grandmaster upon election must go to Warsaw to do homage to the King of Poland. The Knights "must love those whom Poland loved and hate those whom Poland hated." They could have no independent foreign policy of their own. The Prussian nobles and towns could always appeal to the King of Poland for confirmation of their privileges against the rule of the Order.

Albert of Hohenzollern, Duke of Prussia (1525–1568)

Nearly half a century after the Second Peace of Thorn, the greatly weakened Teutonic Knights sought to regain power by choosing as Grandmasters the younger sons of powerful territorial princes in Germany. They hoped thus to get money and troops for aid against Poland. In 1511, partly with this in mind, they elected Albert of Hohenzollern, grandson of Albert Achilles and cousin of Joachim I of Brandenburg. Counting on the assistance of his relatives and on Emperor Maximilian whom he had once aided in a campaign in Italy, he defied the Poles in 1519 and declared war. But he was disappointed in his allies, defeated by the Poles, and forced to make peace.

Meanwhile Lutheranism had begun to spread among the people of Prussia. Albert himself became secretly interested in it, though still protesting publicly his loyalty to Catholicism. In 1523 he visited Luther at Wittenberg. Luther advised: "Give up your vow as monk; take a wife; abolish the Order; and make yourself hereditary Duke of Prussia." Albert was silent for a few minutes; then burst out laughing. It amused him that he had been chosen Grandmaster to strengthen the Order and that now he was advised to abolish it. Yet this is precisely what he proceeded to do. He entered into negotiations with his Polish overlord and secured his consent.

By the Treaty of Cracow with Poland in 1525 the Teutonic Order was dissolved in Prussia and its possessions were transformed into a hereditary duchy for Albert and his descendants, as vassals of the King of Poland. The treaty was approved by the Estates of Prussia. Albert then proceeded to Cracow, took the oath of homage as Duke of Prussia, and received a banner with the Prussian black eagle.

Albert I (1525–1568) began his rule energetically by introducing the Lutheran organization everywhere in Prussia and by showing a real interest in the Renaissance. He was the personal friend of the painter Lucas Cranach and Albrecht Dürer, and of the sculptor Peter Vischer. He founded at Königsberg a printing press, a library, and in 1544 the famous *Albertina,* or university. But in his later years he became indolent, fell into the hands of favorites, and was forced to make such wide concessions to the Estates, representing the Prussian nobles and towns, that he was stripped of a large part of his ducal power.

John Sigismund (1608–1619) : Ruler in Brandenburg, Cleves-Mark, and Prussia

Albert's son and successor Albert Frederick (1568–1618) had a long and miserable existence. Early signs of feeblemindedness gradually developed into serious mental derangement; fits of moroseness and refusal to take food for fear of being poisoned alternated with a feverish fondness for gaiety in dancing and drinking and pommeling his servants. A regency had to be instituted, which was ably administered by his cousin George Frederick of Ansbach from 1577 to the latter's death in 1603, and afterwards by John Sigismund, elector of Brandenburg. Albert Frederick's mental condition made it easy for the Prussian Estates to arrogate to themselves an even greater despotism over the peasants and a still larger control over the government than during the last years of his weak father. The Polish overlord was also always ready to favor the Estates at the expense of the Duke. So it came about that, whereas in Brandenburg the division of power between the prince and the Estates resulted in a kind of "dualism," in Prussia the government virtually passed out of the hands of prince into the control of the narrow-minded and intensely Lutheran Estates, an unfortunate situation that was intensified after John Sigismund turned Calvinist in 1613.

In order to establish a Hohenzollern claim to territories in the valley of the Rhine, Albert Frederick had been betrothed to Mary Eleanor, eldest daughter of William the Rich of Cleves-Jülich. After she set out for Prussia she learned of the mental state of her betrothed; but as she had twice been disappointed in hopes of marriage, she decided not to lose this third chance. She married the crazy duke and bore him numerous children, but only the daughters lived to grow up. The eldest, Anna, married John Sigismund, Elector of Brandenburg, thus giving him a claim to the Cleves-Jülich lands.

The Cleves-Jülich inheritance consisted chiefly of five small duchies and counties: Cleves, Mark, Jülich, Berg, and Ravensberg (*cf.* Shepherd's *Atlas,* maps 114, 122), inhabited by Catholics, Lutherans, and Calvinists. Although not large, their fate, as the extinction of the direct ruling line in 1609, became of great European importance. If they fell to a Protestant, it would aid the Dutch in their struggle for independence against the Spanish Hapsburgs and strengthen the German Protestants in their struggle against the Counter-Reformation. If they fell to a Catholic, they would form an easy connecting link between the Spanish Hapsburgs in the Netherlands and the lands of the Austrian Hapsburgs in the Upper Rhine and Danube valleys. Henry IV of France, James I of England, the Dutch, and the Protestant Union, mainly composed of German Calvinists, were therefore inclined to support the Protestant claimants. The Pope, the Hapsburgs at Vienna and Madrid, and the German Catholic League, led by the Duke of Bavaria, favored a Catholic ruler. There was danger that the question might lead to a general European war.

The principal claimants were: John Sigismund of Brandenburg, a Lutheran; the Duke of Neuburg, a Calvinist; and the Emperor who claimed the lands as escheated fiefs of the Empire and sent Archduke Leopold with an armed force to seize Jülich.

In the face of this Catholic danger John Sigismund and the Duke of Neuburg pooled their Protestant interests and agreed to exercise a joint rule. With the aid of French troops, sent in spite of the assassination of Henry IV, they expelled Archduke Leopold from Jülich. But the condominium did not work smoothly. Friction between the possessory princes was inevitable. Hard words, after heavy drinking, took place between them. Though Carlyle's picturesque story of Neuburg turning from Calvinism to Catholicism because John Sigismund boxed the Duke of Neuburg's ears is pure legend, it is true that in 1613 the two men quarreled. Neuburg, finding little support from the Protestant Union in Germany, then turned Catholic, married the sister of the Catholic Duke Maximilian of Bavaria, and sought the help of his Catholic League.

Six months later John Sigismund turned Calvinist. Since his youth he had been favorably impressed by the Calvinists and their Heidelberg catechism. Two of his best friends and wisest councilors, Herr von Rheydt and Abraham Dohna, were Calvinists and enjoyed close relations with the Orange family in the Netherlands. On the

other hand, his father, his wife, and his Brandenburg and
Prussian Estates were so vehemently Lutheran that he was
deterred from an open change of faith until 1613, when
his sincere religious motives were reinforced by the political consideration that as a Calvinist he might more easily
get the Calvinists in the Netherlands, France, and the
German Protestant Union to back him in his claims to
the Cleves-Jülich inheritance. Whether he was primarily
actuated by the religious or the political motive is less
important than the fact that henceforth the Hohenzollerns
widened their political horizon westward by establishing
closer contact with the more progressive Dutch Reformed
and the French Huguenots, and ceased to be of the same
faith as the great majority of their own Lutheran subjects
in Brandenburg and Prussia. Consequently John Sigismund accompanied his adoption of Calvinism with the
announcement that he would make no use of his right,
cujus regio, ejus religio, but that all his subjects might
enjoy religious freedom—a noteworthy example of toleration in an age of intolerance.

The Cleves-Jülich inheritance question was settled next
year by a compromise: in the Treaty of Xanten of 1614
John Sigismund took over the administration of Cleves,
Mark, and Ravensberg, and the Duke of Neuburg that
of Jülich and Berg; but both princes still reserved their
legal claims to all the lands. Half a century later, in
1666, this provisional division of 1614 was made final.

In the east John Sigismund made an even more important territorial gain. At the death of the crazy old Duke
of Prussia, Albert Frederick, and in accord with earlier
family agreements, the Elector of Brandenburg became
Duke of Prussia in 1618, and as such became a vassal of
the King of Poland.

John Sigismund's reign, bringing Brandenburg, Cleves-
Mark, and Prussia under one ruler, gave to the Hohenzollerns the prospect of a brilliant future. The widely

separated lands foreshadowed the future territorial out-
line of the later Kingdom of Prussia. It became the ambition of his successors to link them together by acquiring
the intervening territory. The union of the three territories, to be sure, was only personal and not organic; that
is, each territory still retained its own separate organization and institutions and tried to pursue its own local
selfish policies. It remained for the later Hohenzollerns
to transform the personal into an organic union, extend-
ing many Brandenburg institutions over the other lands,
and thus creating a unified and centralized state, in which
the single will of the Prince was far stronger and more
enlightened than the narrow separatist tendencies of the
local Estates.

Hardly had John Sigismund succeeded in uniting the
three streams of territory when all Germany began to be
scourged by the terrible Thirty Years' War.

C H A P T E R . . . 2

The Reign
of the Great Elector
(1640–1688)

The Thirty Years' War (1618–1648), beginning at the
moment when John Sigismund's union of Brandenburg,
Cleves, and Prussia had seemed to open such a fair prospect for the Hohenzollerns, caused indescribable devastation and delayed all organic reforms for more than
two decades.

His son and successor George William (1619–1640),
weak, vacillating, and easily influenced, was not at all the
kind of man to face successfully the trying times when
Germany was torn by civil war and trampled upon by
foreign enemies. In each of his three territories powerful
Estate bodies controlled most of the revenues, yet would
raise no troops, except occasionally a few for local use
under the command of their own officers. As George William had almost no available money, he could not hire
soldiers; consequently he could command no respect and
could have no effective foreign policy.

Throughout his reign George William was torn between conflicting factions. His Privy Council, containing Lutherans, Calvinists, and a Catholic, was bitterly divided against itself, until the Catholic Adam von Schwartzenberg managed to oust his opponents and make himself virtually dictator. George William himself was a Calvinist and had married a sister of Frederick V of the Palatinate, the unfortunate "Winter King." But his domineering mother Anna of Prussia and almost all his subjects were fanatically Lutheran, as bitterly opposed to Calvinism as to Catholicism. So the helpless Elector, caught in the storm of the Thirty Years' War, tried in turn three different policies—neutrality, alliance with the Lutheran Swedes, and alliance with the Catholic imperialists—each of which inflicted untold misery and misfortune on his lands.

In allying with the Catholics after 1635, Schwartzenberg hoped to raise an army of 26,000 men, expel the Swedes, and make good the Elector's claim to Pomerania, where the last duke had died without direct heirs in 1637. In fact he was able to raise only 11,000. Even these were so disorderly and disobedient that they not only failed to occupy Pomerania, but were unable to prevent the towns in northern Brandenburg from being treated in terrible fashion by the Swedes. In 1638 George William, discouraged and suffering from an old injury to his leg, was carried in a litter from Berlin to greater safety in Königsberg. Schwartzenberg, remaining behind as virtual dictator in Brandenburg, had grandiose plans for breaking the power of the Estates and building up a strong government in alliance with the Emperor. However, he was universally hated by the Elector's subjects as a traitor and an agent of the Hapsburgs. Moreover, he failed to drive out the Swedes and had enriched himself, while the Elector and those about him were impoverished more and more. His rule, however, was suddenly cut short by death on March 14, 1641. A few weeks earlier George William had also died and been succeeded by his son, Frederick William, an inexperienced youth of twenty who was to win greatness under the well-deserved title of the "Great Elector."

The Great Elector's Youth
(1620–1640)

Frederick William was born in the old Hohenzollern castle at Berlin on February 16, 1620. From his earliest infancy there fell across his life the shadow of the Thirty Years' War. For months he lay unbaptized in his cradle, because there was no money for the baptismal festivities and because no suitable godparents could be secured. At the age of seven, when Wallenstein's soldiers threatened the Electorate, he was transferred from the insecurity of Berlin to the strong fortress of Küstrin and placed under an excellent tutor. Though always holding firmly to the Calvinist teachings of his parents and tutor, he respected, like his grandfather, John Sigismund, the religious convictions of others. His tolerance in an age of intolerance was one of his noblest characteristics and, incidentally, was to prove of great material advantage to his country. He later refused to turn Lutheran to secure the throne of Sweden, or Catholic to secure that of Poland. It was genuine reverence and religious feeling that made him at the age of fourteen choose as his lifemotto the words of the Psalmist:

> Cause me to know the way wherein I should walk;
> For I lift up my soul to thee.

His progress in his studies was satisfactory but not remarkable. He showed good aptitude in drawing, geography, applied mathematics, mechanics, and languages. His first letter to his father, written at the age of seven and thanking him for a horse, was in French, which he learned to write and speak with ease. The same was true of Dutch. He was given a couple of Polish playmates so that he might learn more easily the language of his future Polish overlord. He early developed a hobby for collecting books, engravings, plants, coins, and all sorts of curios, which in riper years led to the founding at Berlin of a library, museum, and model horticultural garden. Fond of bodily exercise, he early learned to ride, fence, fight, and snare birds and rabbits. At twelve he shot his first deer, and in later life became famous for his skill and endurance in hunting the wolves, bears, stags, and wild boars with which his lands abounded.

At fourteen, while the war continued to rage in Germany, Frederick William was sent to study in the stimulating atmosphere of Holland. He listened to lectures at the University of Leyden, famous in physics and mechanics. He delighted in visits to his Orange relatives, his maternal grandmother being a daughter of the great William the Silent. Whether or not Frederick William directly inherited characteristics from the famous Dutch statesman and general one cannot say; but at any rate he resembled him in some of his noblest qualities. At the camp of his great-uncle Frederick Henry of Orange, who was continuing the fight for Dutch independence against the Spanish, he saw the art of war developed by one of the ablest captains of the age. In long letters to his father describing the campaigns and illustrating them with sketches, the future victor of the battles of Warsaw and Fehrbellin already gave evidence of keen interest and military insight. At Frederick Henry's headquarters he also met many of the leading statesmen of the day and learned something of diplomacy. He talked with John Maurice of Nassau, who had organized a colony in Brazil, and was thrilled by the accounts of distant lands and riches overseas. But what most impressed his practical mind was the advanced agricultural methods of the Dutch, their wealth from shipbuilding and trade, their excellent canals, their art and architecture, and their generally high level of intelligence and culture. All these things remained lively memories, refreshed later by the employment of many Hollanders; they stirred ambitions that later ripened with rich advantage to his own more backward lands.

Frederick William also visited Cleves and made such a good impression on the Estates that they begged the Elector to appoint him Governor of Cleves. Frederick William eagerly supported their plea. But George William, more and more under the influence of Schwartzenberg, and fearing his son was becoming too independent, ordered him home. Frederick William was loath to leave the land where he had spent four such happy and profitable years. Delaying his departure on various pretexts for several months, he finally returned to Berlin in 1638. After dining with Schwartzenberg, he suddenly fell sick with a fever and rash. To his dying day he believed that Schwartzenberg, whose policies he hated and whom he believed to be responsible for his recall from Holland, had tried to poison him. Probably, however, he had only had an attack of measles. He spent the next two years at Königsberg in melancholy inactivity, because his father, at Schwartzenberg's advice, refused to initiate him into any government business, and thus deprived him of an opportunity of training for the duties that were soon to fall to him. Finally, on December 1, 1640, George William died of dropsy at forty-six, and "the new master" took the reins.

End of the Thirty Years' War
(1640–1648)

How discouraging was the prospect that faced the youthful Elector! All his territories were more or less occupied by foreign forces. Swedish soldiers held the northern part of Brandenburg and were fighting to conquer the rest of it from the allied troops of Schwartzenberg and the Emperor. The Swedes were also firmly established in the whole of Pomerania, and the Emperor was inclined to let them keep it in disregard of Brandenburg's just claim to it. In Prussia the Swedish toll collectors had withdrawn, but their place had been taken by Poles. In Cleves-Mark many of the towns were in the hands of the Dutch, the Imperialists, or the Hessians. Even more distressing to a prince who held absolutist views was the fact that in each of his territories the Elector's authority had vanished to a shadow before the selfish "privileges" of the local Estates. He had no available revenues and no dependable troops with which to assert his authority at home or abroad.

Furthermore, the ravages of war had wrought terrible ruin. Battle, murder, starvation, and suicide had swept away more than half the population of Brandenburg. Fields went out of cultivation; roads and bridges were impassable; clipped and counterfeit coins drove out good money; and commerce decayed. Berlin, which had frequently ransomed itself from complete destruction by heavy payments had only 6000 inhabitants in 1640 compared with 14,000 in 1618, Frankfort on the Oder 2000 instead of 12,000, and Prenzlau on the Pomeranian frontier 600 instead of 9000! The open unfortified peasant villages suffered even more severely than the towns. Hundreds had been burned to the ground and become a wilderness for wolves, the peasants having been completely exterminated. The total number of the Great Elector's subjects at his accession had shrunk from about 1,500,000 before the war to hardly 600,000 souls, about 240,000 in Brandenburg (including the New Mark), 260,000 in Prussia, and 100,000 in Cleves, Mark, and Ravensberg. Thus his total population in 1640 was no larger than that of a good-sized American city of today, such as Buffalo or

Milwaukee. But by his death in 1688 he had much more than doubled it—to about 1,500,000—partly by acquiring new lands, partly by settling new colonists, and partly by the relatively great prosperity that he introduced.

Realizing his weakness from lack of money and dependable troops, Frederick William began his reign prudently by gently conciliating his enemies at home and abroad. Instead of dismissing the hated Schwartzenberg, as was generally expected, the Elector left him as Governor of Brandenburg until the rioting of Schwartzenberg's own disorderly soldiery conveniently frightened him to death four months later. The Elector reinstated at once, however, the Lutheran and Calvinist councilors whom Schwartzenberg had forced out of the Privy Council, and appointed some young and energetic friends of his own, like Conrad von Burgsdorf, and a little later Blumenthal, Waldeck, and Schwerin. He adopted the wise practice which he later recommended to his son in his characteristic advice of 1667:

In council give earnest attention. Note well the opinions of all the councilors, and also have a careful record kept. In matters which are important and where secrecy is necessary, make no final decision in the presence of the councilors, but take the question home to think over; afterwards have one or another of the Privy Councilors and a secretary come to you; think over again all the opinions which were expressed, and make then your own decision. Be like the bee, which sucks the sweetest juice from all the flowers. If it is a difficult question, pray God that He will enlighten your heart as to what you must do or leave undone, in order that it may be for the honor of His name and of your lands and peoples and subjects, and also to the best advantage of yourself and your house.

To secure the goodwill of his Polish overlord, the young Elector journeyed to Warsaw, knelt before Ladislas IV, and was invested with the Duchy of Prussia. He further promised to permit the construction of Catholic churches, to pay an annual tribute, and to exclude Calvinists from office in Prussia. Having thus strengthened himself against Polish interference, he returned to Königsberg and secured the homage of the Prussian Estates by confirming their traditional privileges.

Meanwhile Conrad von Burgsdorf had been despatched to Brandenburg to relieve the Electorate from the double scourge of Schwartzenberg's soldiery and the Swedish attacks. The troops that Schwartzenberg hired in alliance with the Emperor had, as he himself complained, mostly been "blown away like scum on the sea." Though less than 5000 remained, he had made a last effort to drive back the Swedes in order to justify his pro-Austrian policy. It not only failed completely, but stirred the Swedes to retaliate by advancing against Berlin. One of Schwartzenberg's last and most hated acts was his burning some of the houses outside the walls lest they afford a shelter for the enemy's attack. The new master in Königsberg, however, sent orders to stand strictly on the defensive as a preliminary to negotiations for an armistice. Without sufficient troops to expel the Swedes, he believed it wiser to negotiate with them. This would also make it possible for him to reduce Schwartzenberg's disorderly soldiery, as he had been urgently begged to do by a delegation from the Brandenburg Estates. An armistice with the Swedes and a reduction of troops were to go hand in hand.

The remnants of Schwartzenberg's soldiery (*soldatesca*) represented the worst scum of Europe. As was customary in the Thirty Years' War, they had been recruited under the old regimental mercenary system, in which the colonel received a lump sum for raising and equipping a regiment, which he regarded as his own private property. Only when it was mustered for review by the prince who was paying for it would the colonel make frantic attempts

to show a full regiment. Usually he did so only by resort-
ing to devious frauds, such as making the same soldier
pass in review several times, borrowing soldiers tempo-
rarily from brother colonels, or enrolling ruffians and
hangers-on hastily gathered at the moment. Colonel
Klitzing, for example, who had received 40,000 talers from
Schwartzenberg for supposedly 2200 soldiers, actually had
on foot less than 100. A colonel, having pocketed his
money, often defied the prince whom he had sworn to
serve and plundered the people he was supposed to protect. He was as tyrannical over his ruffian soldiers as over
the cowering civilian population. For small offenses he
flogged them, branded them, sliced off their ears and
noses, and compelled them to endure the torture of running the gauntlet. Several of these unruly colonels refused to obey orders from the new Elector. One of them,
after browbeating the pastor and citizens of Spandau,
defiantly threatened to blow up the fortress and set fire
to the town he was paid to defend. The population of
Brandenburg complained bitterly that the soldier within
the gates was far more terrible than the Swede without,
and renewed their prayer to Frederick William that he
disband the unruly *soldatesca.*

Conrad von Burgsdorf therefore proceeded energetically against Schwartzenberg's colonels. Some were arrested; others fled; a few loyal ones were retained and
took a new oath to the Elector alone but not to the Emperor as heretofore. From the men in the ranks were
dropped the undesirable and the unfit. From one regiment,
for instance, Burgsdorf purged thirty-three native-born
Swedes; thirty-two Scotch, Irish, and Polish adventurers;
and thirty men "crooked, lame, and useless."

Those who were retained in service numbered less than
2500, merely enough to garrison the fortresses. But they
formed a tiny nucleus for a new and relatively well-
disciplined army. It was composed so far as possible of

the Great Elector's own subjects, so that it might feel that it was fighting for the defense of home and country. It was sufficiently well paid so that it did not have to resort to the plunder and oppression of the people it was supposed to protect, and it was soon decently uniformed in blue. In the last years of the Thirty Years' War it was gradually increased to nearly 8000 men, partly supported by grants from the grateful Estates, and was a decisive factor in winning for Frederick William respectful consideration in the long negotiations leading to the Peace of Westphalia.

By excluding the Imperialists from Brandenburg, Frederick William succeeded in making an armistice with the Swedes in July 1641. Swedish troops were to remain in occupation of six towns and were to be allowed peaceful passage through the Electorate, but otherwise Frederick William regained control of his Brandenburg lands and relieved them from further devastation. The armistice was for a term of two years, but was later extended until the final peace in 1648.

The armistice, however, did not include Pomerania, which remained completely in Swedish hands. To secure this and to establish sea power on the Baltic, Frederick William secretly sought the hand of Queen Christina of Sweden. She, however, like Queen Elizabeth of England, had no intention of binding herself to a husband. So Frederick William finally abandoned this hope, and in 1646 sought an alliance with the Dutch by marrying Louise Henrietta, the daughter of Frederick Henry of Orange. Small in stature, tender and devoted, she proved an excellent wife until her death in 1667. The pleasant castle of Oranienburg, some thirty miles north of Berlin, named in her honor, became one of the favorite residences of the young couple.

At the long peace negotiations to end the Thirty Years' War, which took place from 1644 to 1648 at Münster and Osnabrück in Westphalia, Frederick William was not personally present. But through his delegates he strove energetically to secure primarily two things: legal recognition for his coreligionists, the Calvinists (or Reformed, as they were generally called), and the possession of the whole of Pomerania.

In his first aim he was successful, in spite of the opposition of the Lutherans who set up an even more determined opposition than the Catholics. By the Treaty of Westphalia Calvinists were given the same legal recognition in the Empire that Lutherans and Catholics had enjoyed since the Peace of Augsburg of 1555. Largely through his influence there was added also the tolerant provision that no prince should henceforth make use of his *jus reformandi,* his right of compelling conformity by expelling subjects who differed in religion from himself.

In the Pomeranian question, however, he was less successful. It was generally admitted that by earlier treaties he had a just claim to the whole of Pomerania after the death of the last duke in 1637. But the Swedes were in occupation and claimed it as one of the spoils of war; otherwise they would not make peace. The Emperor and most of the German princes were inclined to let them keep it to get rid of them, even at the sacrifice of the Elector's rights. But with the support of the French and the Dutch, Frederick William finally secured a compromise. Pomerania was partitioned. The Swedes kept Western or Hither Pomerania, including the valuable port of Stettin; the mouth of the Oder; and a strip of territory along its east bank. Frederick William was given Eastern or Further Pomerania with the less good port of Colberg. To compensate him for the rest of his claim, he was also given several secularized bishoprics: Cammin, adjoining Pomerania on the east; Minden on the Weser, serving as a link toward the eventual connection of Brandenburg and Revensberg to the west; Halberstadt; and the expectancy to the great Bishopric of Magdeburg (possession upon the death of the Saxon incumbent, which occurred in 1680). All these new lands, especially Halberstadt and Magdeburg that rounded out the Electorate to the southeast, greatly strengthened the growing importance of the Hohenzollerns. Next to the Hapsburgs, they had become the strongest ruling family in Germany.

The Northern War (1655–1660)

The Thirty Years' War was followed by seven years of peace (1648–1655), but not of perfect calm. The unexecuted clauses of the Treaty of Westphalia, the continuance of war between France and Spain, and the increasing hostility between Sweden and Poland caused a feeling of general insecurity that made the peace little better than an armed truce. Nevertheless, Frederick William was able to begin some of the remarkable reforms that will be described in a later section. He was unfortunately interrupted in this by the war between Sweden and Poland.

In 1654 Queen Christina of Sweden wearied of shocking Europe by reveling in masculine clothes and oaths and by performing feats in horsemanship and hunting. Giving Europe a new thrill, she suddenly abdicated the throne of Gustavus Adolphus, abjured Lutheranism, and lived for some thirty years, more picturesquely than piously, as a Roman Catholic in the Eternal City. The crown of Sweden fell to her warlike and ambitious cousin Charles. In one of his first council meetings he urged that Sweden needed to make war as a means of drawing out of the country the lazy and disorderly soldiery who had returned from the Thirty Years' War and had become a plague in the land. Passing in review the countries whom he might attack, Charles X picked on Poland; his family had dynastic claims to Poland, and the conquest of Poland

would enable him to carry out the Swedish dream of turning the Baltic into a Swedish lake. In July 1655 Swedish
troops unceremoniously marched across the Great Elector's territory of Eastern Pomerania to attack Poland.

Faced with this danger of the Northern War upon his
borders, without any considerable troops on hand of his
own, and unable to count on effective cooperation from
any of the European powers, Frederick William was in a
perilous position. He was in danger of being engulfed in
the war and of losing Prussia and Pomerania. He saw
three courses open to him: (1) He might adopt neutrality,
in spite of Machiavelli's dictum that it is folly for a
prince to be neutral when his neighbors fall to fighting
and so to run the risk of being later overwhelmed by the
victor. (2) He might join the Swedes, and with their help
hope to throw off the Polish overlordship over East Prussia and to conquer Polish West Prussia, thus consolidating
Brandenburg, Eastern Pomerania, and Prussia into a solid
block of connected territory. (3) Or he might fight on the
side of Poland, in accordance with his legal obligation as
a vassal of the Polish king, and hope to conquer Swedish
(Western) Pomerania which he failed to get at the Peace
of Westphalia. His councilors were divided in opinion as
between these alternatives. Frederick William therefore
followed his own judgment. He adopted a skillful but
unscrupulous opportunism, justified only, if at all, by
the difficulties of his situation and the success with which
he extricated himself. He proceeded to adopt one after
another all three of the above alternative courses!

To command respect for his first policy, that of neutrality, Frederick William's prime need was a sizeable
army. Aside from his modest military escort of 63 horse
guards and 202 life guards, his Lilliputian army of 4000
was barely sufficient to garrison his widely scattered fortresses, let alone being utterly inadequate to defend the
frontiers against fighting Poles and Swedes. He there-

fore had his officers begin at once to recruit a regular army in the Cleves and Brandenburg territories and called out the militia in East Prussia. By September 1655 he had an army of 8000; by June 1656, 18,000; and by the end of the war, 27,000.

The Brandenburg Estates at first refused to grant any money for the support of these troops. They declared that Brandenburg was not in direct danger from the Poles or Swedes; that they were under no obligations to defend Frederick William's other lands; if East Prussia was in danger, let it look out for its own safety. To this parochial view the Elector replied with characteristic breadth of outlook, July 12, 1655:

The military preparations of all our neighbors compel us to follow their example. And since this army is for the benefit not simply of one, but of all my lands, I deem it proper that the cost and maintenance of the troops must be borne by all my lands, and that the soldiery must be assigned among them proportionally.

When the Estates still refused, preferring "to trust in God and wait patiently upon events," Frederick William proceeded to the extreme step of collecting a land tax of 180,000 talers by military execution. After this sign of his determination, the Estates "with much lamenting" granted considerable sums for the maintenance of the army during the Northern War.

Meanwhile Charles X had marched victoriously into Poland. The fickle Poles quickly recognized him as king, and their own ruler John Casimir fled the country. After a few months, however, the brutality of the Swedish soldiers and their desecration of Catholic churches and monasteries brought about a new revulsion of Polish feeling. A national Polish uprising against the invader and the return of John Casimir forced Charles X back to the frontier of Prussia. Wishing to avoid a conflict with the Brandenburg-Prussian troops, he was glad to enter into negotiations. So Frederick William turned from neutrality to alliance with Sweden. By the Treaty of Königsberg (January 17, 1656) he established friendship with Charles X and recognized him, instead of John Casimir, as King of Poland and therefore as his overlord in East Prussia; and by the Treaty of Marienburg (June 25) he made a definite alliance, joined his army with that of the Swedes, and was promised in return a considerable slice of Poland when it should be conquered. To conquer this and to suppress the Polish national uprising Charles X and Frederick William then marched together toward the Polish capital. In the great three-day Battle of Warsaw (July 28–30) the allied force of 18,000 put to rout 70,000 undisciplined Polish troops. For the first time soldiers of Brandenburg, Prussia, and Cleves-Mark fought side by side under a single flag and a single leader for a single common purpose—the strengthening of the dynastic power of the Hohenzollern family. The new army, which strikingly embodied the new Brandenburg-Prussian state, had borne gloriously its first baptism of fire.

The Battle of Warsaw, however, was more glorious than advantageous. The capture of the Polish capital did not mean the end of the war. Pestilence broke out in the allied armies and they were compelled to retreat into Prussia. Here Frederick William was able to force Charles X, as the price of his continuing the alliance, by the Treaty of Labiau (November 26) to abandon the overlordship and recognize him as sovereign in Prussia. It now only remained for him to force John Casimir to do likewise.

The death of the Emperor Ferdinand III on April 2, 1657, his son's desire to secure the Brandenburg vote at the imperial election, and the skillful intrigues of the Hapsburg diplomatist Lisola paved the way for Frederick

William's third political somersault. By the Treaty of Wehlau (September 19, 1657), he allied with Poland against Sweden, and was promised that he should rule in full sovereignty (*jure supremi domini*) in East Prussia and receive some minor territorial gains. A little later he allied with the Emperor also, with the aim of driving the Swedes out of Germany altogether. While his Catholic allies conquered part of Swedish Pomerania, Frederick William's army defeated the Swedish force that had occupied the Danish lands.

But as the Northern War became more general, France, England, and the Dutch put pressure on the allies to make peace. The sudden death of Charles X afforded a favorable opportunity. By the general peace signed on May 3, 1660, at the monastery of Oliva, on the shore of the Baltic, north of Danzig, Frederick William finally won "his best jewel"—the prize that he had ever kept before his mind during the tortuous diplomacy of the Northern War— namely, the recognition by his neighbors of his sovereignty in Prussia. The humiliating Polish overlordship that had existed since 1466, as well as the temporary Swedish overlordship of 1656, was at an end. Since Prussia was not a part of the Holy Roman Empire, Frederick William had raised himself above his fellow German princes, who theoretically were under the Emperor; by the strength of his army and by his new position in Prussia he had elevated himself to the rank of a European sovereign. But would his own Prussian subjects recognize him as sovereign?

The Struggle for Absolutism

War almost inevitably leads to a great increase in the activity and power of the prince or the central government. Military efficiency necessitates increased taxes; and increased taxes mean new methods, new officials, and

more centralized administrative institutions. So it happened that the Thirty Years' War, and especially the
Northern War, aided the Great Elector in building up a
more unified administration and in establishing his absolutism at the expense of the Estates, thus doing away
with the paralyzing "dualism" caused by the concessions
extorted by the nobles and towns from his predecessors.

During the Thirty Years' War Schwartzenberg had
forcibly collected military taxes over the protest of the
Estates and had set up a War Council (*Kriegsrat*) of his
own that effectually usurped the place of the Privy Council. By so doing, as well as by his pro-Catholic policy, he
had aroused the intense hatred of the nobles and towns.
The Great Elector, on the other hand, began his reign by
trying to conciliate his Brandenburg subjects. The War
Council was abolished and the Privy Council was restored.
The armistice with the Swedes made possible a reduction
of the *soldatesca* and military taxes. His requests to the
Estates to grant money to increase the tiny force of 4000
troops maintained after the Peace of Westphalia led to
long hagglings, which resulted in a few small grants by
the Estates and some further military collections by the
Elector.

Finally, in 1653, in view of the threatening conditions
all over Europe, the Brandenburg Estates were persuaded
to make a grant of 530,000 talers, to be paid in six annual
installments, 59 percent being raised by the towns and
the remaining 41 percent by the nobles (from their peasants). The Estates of course expected that after the six-
year grant was exhausted they would be called together
again whenever the Elector needed more money. In 1659,
however, the Northern War was still going on and Frederick William simply continued to collect the indispensable taxes without any further grant by the Estates. So the
Diet of 1653 was the last which ever met in Brandenburg
(although local diets, performing mostly ceremonial func-

tions, survived until the nineteenth century). The central body was succeeded by a committee (formerly of fifty, and later of twelve, deputies) whose chief task was to manage the old financial machinery (*Kreditwerk*) that had been established to take care of Joachim II's debts and that existed until Hardenberg's financial reform in 1821.

More important than the elimination of the Diet as an obstacle to the Elector's absolutism was the shrewd and skillful manner in which he transformed certain officials representing the rival power of the Diet into loyal and devoted agents of his own absolutist authority. Long before the Thirty Years' War the Estates met not only in a general Diet for the whole Electorate, but also in local assemblies (*Kreistage*) in the twenty-odd districts or "circles" into which Brandenburg and the New Mark were divided. Here they nominated one or more directors for each district (*Kreisdirectores*) to look after their corporate interests in general, and in particular to supervise the collection of the nonmilitary taxes granted by the general Diet. These consisted mainly of the old land tax (*Hufenschoss*) raised by the nobles from their peasants, and the beer tax raised by the towns.

During the Thirty Years' War, when foreign troops were overrunning Brandenburg and when the Elector had to raise, feed, and quarter troops of his own, he began to appoint local agents to aid him and to protect as far as possible the rights and property of his subjects. These agents were variously known as War Commissars (*Kriegskommissare* or *Marschkommissare*) or as District Commissars (*Kreiskommissare*), there being one, or more often two, for each district. They received and supervised the money granted by the Estates for military purposes, or, if this was insufficient, levied money and provisions by military execution. They conducted troops on the march through their district, assigned them quarters, regulated the supply of food and fodder, and sought to restrain as

far as possible "insolence" and plundering by the *soldatesca*. They exercised a kind of police power. Their task
was not easy: they sometimes had to make provision out
of their own pocket and one was cudgeled for his pains.
No wonder they were often reluctant to accept appointment or asked to be released from office. Nevertheless,
they helped save their districts from an otherwise more
dreadful fate. In selecting them, frequently upon the
nomination of the district nobles themselves, the Elector
was often shrewd enough to appoint as War Commissars
the very nobles who were already serving as elected District Directors. The point is often argued by Prussian
historians whether the War Commissar represented the
Elector or the Estates. The fact is he represented both.
He was an appointee of the Elector and was a prime factor in building up the standing army, which came to be
the symbol of unity and strength in the Hohenzollern
state. At the same time he had at heart the interests of
his district and brother nobles, was usually a man of their
choice (if he happened to be a *Kreisdirector*), and received
a small compensation paid by them. In the second half
of the seventeenth century he came to exercise increased
police and judicial powers, acquired social prestige, and
after 1702 rejoiced in the title of County Magistrate
(*Landrat*). This officer, introduced from Brandenburg
into the other Hohenzollern lands, remained ever after
the chief local administrative officer in the rural districts,
an invaluable agent of the central government, and a
loyal and devoted servant of the Hohenzollern dynasty.

The *new* land tax (*Kontribution*), granted for military
purposes by the Estates during and immediately after the
Thirty Years' War, but collected by the Elector after 1659
without any grant, was supervised by the War Commissars. As the private demesne lands of the nobles were
exempt from this, and as he had had to haggle with the
Estates to get it granted at all, the Great Elector had

intended to supplement or replace it with a general assessment (*Assise* or *Akzise*) on consumption goods. This recently invented tax had proved a financial gold mine in France and Holland as he had observed. Being an indirect tax and not demandable on any fixed date, its collection would be less noticed and opposed. It had the further advantage that the nobles would have to pay it, though of course the burden on them would be relatively much less than on the poorer classes. Just because it threatened their "privilege" of tax-exemption, the nobles successfully thwarted its general adoption. The Brandenburg towns, however, soon came to find it a very convenient way of raising their quota (59 percent) of the military tax and began to adopt it. At first it was collected by the town magistrates; after 1682 it became an obligatory state tax collected in the towns by War-tax Commissars (*Steuerkommissare*) appointed by the Elector. These officials of the central government gradually took over the whole town administration in the name of the Elector, thus depriving the towns of the oligarchic self-government and political power which they had enjoyed since the Middle Ages. The end result of the various policies of the Great Elector was the establishment of absolutism based upon three important instruments: an enlarged army, new taxes to support it, and new officials to carry the authority of the central government into the rural districts and urban centers.

In Cleves-Mark the Estates resisted the Elector more successfully than in Brandenburg. Far removed from the center in Berlin, they got the backing of the Netherlands and the Duke of Neuburg in Jülich so long as the Elector's authority remained provisional, that is, until his treaty with Neuburg in 1666. The "privileges" on which they insisted were numerous: annual meetings without any summons or interference by the Elector; an oath of loyalty to their laws instead of to the Elector by all officials; no taxes, nor recruiting and garrisoning of troops, nor building of defense fortresses, nor even bringing in Electoral troops, except by consent of the Estates; and especially the "right of the native born" (*Indigenatsrecht*), by which the Elector could appoint no official in Cleves-Mark except a person who happened to be so fortunate as to have been born and to own property in the territories.

In spite of these pretensions, Frederick William managed to recruit some 6000 troops in Cleves-Mark during the Northern War. After the war, and especially after 1666, with the promise of Dutch subsidies to prevent the French conquest of the lower Rhine, with his standing army and with his triumph over opposition in Brandenburg, he was able to take a firmer stand. He sent troops into Cleves-Mark and garrisoned them there, and curtailed some of the other privileges. The Estates still retained their right to meet and grant taxes, but soon recognized the standing army as a permanent institution, and made regular and even generous grants for its support, ranging from 110,000 talers in 1661 to 190,000 in 1687. In return the Elector respected the "right of the native born." At the time of his death in 1688 a very satisfactory harmony was established, and Cleves-Mark gradually became organically united with Brandenburg by accepting most of the Elector's centralizing institutions.

The Struggle for Absolutism in Prussia

In East Prussia the conflict with the Estates was more determined and bitter, owing to the peculiar bonds between Prussia and Poland and to the tragic opposition of Roth and Kalckstein. During more than two centuries the Prussian Estates had gradually acquired enormously wide "privileges," largely as a result of their habit of appealing to Poland against their own ruler—first against

the Grandmaster and after 1525 against the Hohenzollern
Dukes of Prussia. The "liberties" of which they boasted
came to resemble the unbridled license of the Polish
nobility, while the ducal power was whittled down almost
to the vanishing point, as in the case of the politically
impotent Polish kings of the seventeenth century. Many
Prussian nobles held office or land in Poland, and could
play a double role—as Poles in Warsaw and as Germans
in Prussia. All Prussian subjects enjoyed since 1466 the
right to carry cases on appeal from the Prussian courts
to the courts of the Polish overlord. The Prussian Estates
wanted to preserve the close bonds with Poland because
they were the bulwark of their "liberties"; for the same
reason the Great Elector wished to sever them. His re-
quest that the Estates recognize him as sovereign brought
to a head a fundamental issue; medieval Polish feudalism
or modern Hohenzollern absolutism; selfish local class
privileges or the common good of the whole state as interpreted by the Elector.

At his accession in 1640, with the Thirty Years' War
on his hands, the Great Elector had prudently confirmed
the privileges of the Estates and so avoided raising the
issue. During the Northern War, to be sure, he had been
forced to levy a general excise tax and to recruit troops,
and the Estates had accepted the exigencies of the situation, though not without protests. In 1660, however, with
his sovereignty recognized in the Treaty of Oliva, and
with his continued taxation and maintenance of troops,
the issue became unavoidable. The Estates claimed that
they were not bound by treaties in which they had not
been consulted and to which they were not a party. They
maintained that treaties affecting Prussia required the free
consent of all three political factors: the King of Poland,
the Duke of Prussia, and the Prussian Estates; that Prussia
and Poland formed a *corpus individuum, quod non sepa-
rari potest;* and that this *nexus in aeternum* could not be

dissolved by two of the parties without the consent of the third. They demanded therefore that the question be laid before a Polish Diet that should be attended by a deputation of the Prussian Estates, and that thus, in the presence of Estates, Elector, and King, new constitutional relations should be agreed upon and adopted.

Unable to come at once in person to Prussia, Frederick William sent his closest friend and wisest counselor, the gentle but firm Otto von Schwerin, to deal with the situation. He found a hostile and treacherous ferment on all sides. The nobles and towns demanded that he call a meeting of the Estates, redress their grievances in connection with the taxes and troops levied during the Northern War, and confirm all their ancient privileges.

The leading spirits among the nobles were Albert von Kalckstein and his son Christian Ludwig. The father had enriched himself in Saxon military service during the Thirty Years' War and acquired considerable property in Prussia and Lusatia. In 1657 he had taken part in a conspiracy with Poland against the Elector's authority in Prussia. After the Treaty of Oliva he secretly joined with others in sending a letter urging Polish troops to reoccupy Prussia. His unfortunate son Christian Ludwig von Kalckstein had served in the French army under Turenne until dismissed as a disorderly character. He entered the Polish army in 1654, but in the Northern War raised a regiment for the Great Elector, fought on his side at the Battle of Warsaw, and was rewarded by the gift of the lucrative captaincy of the Prussian district of Oletzko. In 1659, however, he was accused by the clerk of the district of graft and maltreatment of the inhabitants, and was consequently suspended from his captaincy by order of the Elector. Thenceforth he was filled with the bitterest hatred. He reentered the Polish army, and in 1661 was in Warsaw furthering his father's efforts to persuade the Poles to prevent Frederick William from establishing his sovereignty in Prussia.

Hieronymus Roth was of more estimable personal character and even more determined in his opposition to the Elector's sovereignty. As a member of the powerful Merchants' Gild in Königsberg and a leading town magistrate with the arts and convictions of a demagogue, he incited opposition in the towns. He kept in touch with Poland through his brother, a Jesuit in Warsaw, as well as by occasional visits by himself or his son to Polish magnates.

In May 1661 Schwerin summoned the Estates—the "Great Diet"—which sat with interruptions from 1661 to 1663. Its debates and proceedings fill three large volumes. Schwerin made a conciliatory proposal to confirm most of the privileges in return for recognition of the Elector's sovereignty. The proposal was at once rejected. In addition to demands similar to those of the Brandenburg and Cleves Estates—regular meetings, no taxes or troops or fortifications except by their consent, the "right of the native born," and oppressive control over the peasantry— the Prussian Diet insisted on protection from competition of French, Scotch, and other foreign traders, exclusion from office of all Calvinists, continuance of the right of appeal to Polish courts, and nonrecognition of the Elector's sovereignty except by a new agreement with Poland in which they should participate.

Early in the session Schwerin perceived that Roth was the chief instigator of the opposition. He therefore invited him to the castle for a private talk. Both men apparently lost their temper. According to Schwerin's account, Roth denounced the Elector as a tyrant and declared that never should he have the sovereignty, so that Schwerin doubted "whether the fellow was *sanae mentis* or filled with brandy." According to his own account, Roth merely quoted a noble who had called the Elector a tyrant, and had only said that he did not know what good the sovereignty would do him if the Estates retained all their privileges.

The conflict with the Estates dragged on for a year and seemed to approach a deadlock. The Lutheran clergy preached against the threatened "slavery"; the building of a Calvinist church in Königsberg was prevented by force; and there was the danger that Poland might actively intervene. Schwerin decided that Roth, as the chief fomenter of trouble, should be arrested. But this was not so easy, as Roth was protected by the people and Schwerin did not have sufficient troops to make it safe to attempt to seize him by force. Moreover, in March 1662 surmising an effort to arrest him, Roth disguised himself as a monk and escaped to talk with the King of Poland. When he slipped back again to Königsberg, eluding the cavalry detachment on watch to pick him up, he kept in hiding. In June his son traveled secretly to Warsaw and urged John Casimir "no longer to permit that we should be crucified in infamous and miserable ways." The King, who wanted to support the Prussians but did not want to risk another war with the Great Elector, gave young Roth a cautiously worded letter. The elder Roth interpreted this as a promise of support. Accordingly, he collected his followers in the cathedral, read them John Casimir's letter, and invited them to swear to a "pledge against the foreign councilors," that is, against Schwerin. However, the oath was not taken on the spot, as the pledge was given over to the gilds to consider.

In this situation Frederick William decided to come in person to Königsberg, bringing with him some two thousand troops that were placed in strategic positions. He was highly indignant against Roth because of his sayings and doings as reported by Schwerin, and agreed that he ought to be arrested if it could be done without bloodshed. A ruse was successful. A small squad of soldiers was marched past the house where Roth was hiding; he put his head out of the window to see what was going on, was recognized, quickly seized, and carried to the castle. Here he was brought to trial before a special commission composed of Prussian nobles and burghers. They found him guilty on five counts, but rejected the death penalty and urged a pardon. Even Schwerin advised his master that it would be wiser to win his subjects by clemency than to frighten them by an example of severity. The Elector, however, believing that Roth had insulted his person by calling him a tyrant and had incited the people against his authority, condemned him to imprisonment for life. On several occasions he intimated that if Roth would acknowledge his error and beg for a pardon it would be granted. Roth, equally determined and obstinate, refused, believing that in opposing the Elector's sovereignty he had constitutional right on his side. So he remained in mild captivity until his death in 1678. At the news of Roth's arrest Albert von Kalckstein, fearing a similar fate, hastily fled.

The Estates, deprived of their chief leaders, impressed by Frederick William's determined attitude, and coaxed by his conciliatory offers, finally yielded in May 1663. They agreed to do homage to him as sovereign, provided Polish deputies were present as a matter of form to release them from their allegiance to Poland. He in return confirmed all their privileges so far as these did not conflict with his sovereign rights. He promised to call a Diet at least every six years; reduced somewhat the taxes and troops; and agreed that the Calvinists should not have more than four churches in Prussia and should only be admitted to a few minor offices. In gaining the essential point of sovereignty, Frederick William had won a triumph for himself personally and for the future of his state.

In 1669 the Estates again refused for months to grant taxes as requested. This renewed opposition contributed to seal the fate of Christian Ludwig von Kalckstein. After his father's death in 1667 he quarreled bitterly with his brother and sisters over the division of the elder Kalckstein's property. In their hatred they denounced him as having boasted of a threat to murder the Elector. At an examination before magistrates he was asserted to have boasted in public that he had planned a Polish invasion of Prussia in which he would burn and plunder; that in revenge for his suspension from the captaincy of Oletzko he would write "Suspended!" on the walls of the ruined Prussian towns; that if he came across the Elector and princes he would spare none but hew down all. So much of the evidence brought against him by his own relatives seemed inspired by family hatred rather than zeal for truth and justice that the court was in doubt until Kalckstein conceived the unhappy idea of bribing two of his servants to take false names and give perjured testimony. This was discovered and made the court doubt the veracity of his denials of the allegations brought by his relatives. Accordingly, he was sentenced to life imprisonment.

When the Elector came to Königsberg six months later, Kalckstein humbly begged for mercy, and the sentence was generously changed from imprisonment for life to the payment of a fine. Instead of paying this he packed his money and valuables on sledges and fled on a winter's night to Warsaw. Here he turned Roman Catholic to curry favor with the Poles, and distributed handbills telling how the Great Elector was maltreating his subjects. All this was too much for Frederick William's patience. When the King of Poland refused to extradite Kalckstein, the Prussian agent in Warsaw managed to kidnap him, roll him in a rug, and hustle him across the frontier back into Prussia. Here in 1671 he was brought to trial a second time, even tortured to make him reveal the accomplices among the Prussian nobility at whom he had hinted, and finally condemned and executed for treason.

After this example of severity the Great Elector met very little further resistance from the Prussian Estates. From 1680 onwards he drew a regular military revenue from Prussia, consisting of a land tax in the rural districts and small towns, and an excise tax in Königsberg. This separate treatment of town and country gave a deathblow to the corporate solidarity of the Estates and contributed to their final disappearance in 1705—except when called to do homage at the accession of a new sovereign.

Shifting Alliances (1660–1688)

Never, except perhaps among the Italians of Machiavelli's day, were alliances so rapidly made and so ruthlessly broken as in the second half of the seventeenth century. In the diplomatic period following the Thirty Years' War religious interests had begun to lose their influence, and the political interest of the state (*Staatsräson*) was becoming increasingly the new and higher guiding rule of conduct of the absolutist princes. No prince was cleverer or more opportunist in this than the Great Elector, partly because of his shrewd practical common sense and determined character, and partly because his lands, scattered from the Meuse to the Memel, touched so many states that his diplomatic position was extremely complicated and precarious.

No brief narrative can give any adequate account of his numerous shifting alliances. Suffice it to say that, from the end of the Northern War to his death in 1688, Frederick William was several times in alliance with England, Holland, France, Denmark, Sweden, Austria, Spain, and various German states, and often allied with several at the same time. Except for brief periods in 1668, 1670, 1673–1674 and from 1679–1686, when he was disgusted with his Dutch and Hapsburg allies and influenced by the hope of generous French subsidies to support his army, his

Protestant sympathies (and also the promise of Dutch subsidies) tended toward alliances with Holland and England to protect the Lower Rhine from the aggression of Louis XIV. As a German prince who received subsidies from the Empire, he was often in alliance with the Hapsburgs in defense of the Holy Roman Empire against the French and the Turks. The kernel of his thought is to be found in the very interesting secret "advice" to his son in 1667:

Alliances, to be sure, are good: but a force of one's own on which one can rely better. A ruler is treated with no consideration if he does not have troops and means of his own. It is these, Thank God! which have made me *considerabel* since the time that I began to have them.

The Great Elector's alliances were mainly defensive but were also partly motivated by the fact that his lands were still too poor to support from his own resources an army large enough to defend his scattered territories and to enable him to follow a wholly independent foreign policy. His alliances therefore were often partly dictated by the hope of subsidies. From 1674 to 1688 these foreign subsidies totaled roughly 2,712,000 talers: 57,000 from Denmark, 467,000 from Spain, 503,000 from France, 912,000 from the Netherlands, and 973,000 from the Empire. As he was able during these years to squeeze only the equivalent of 20,000,000 for military purposes from his own lands, much of which was in the form of deliveries in kind instead of cash, and as he wisely refrained from borrowing heavily (less than 700,000 talers), these cash subsidies represented an important item in building up the army that was to make him "considerable."

War was forced upon the Great Elector a third time by Louis XIV's invasion of Holland in 1672. By treaty the Elector was to aid the Dutch, but he unfortunately sought to do so by marching with a Hapsburg force under Montecuccoli in the Middle instead of the Lower Rhine. The Elector was eager to push forward and divert Turenne from the Dutch, but Montecuccoli refused to cross the Rhine. So the Dutch withheld the promised subsidies, and the Elector, constantly held back by the balky Hapsburg horse to which he was yoked, withdrew for a year from the war. In 1674, with Turenne's invasion of the Palatinate and a declaration of war against the French by the imperial Reichstag, Frederick William again took his place beside the Hapsburg army in defense of the Holy Roman Empire. The allies drove the French back into Alsace and had a good chance to crush Turenne near Colmar, when the Elector's fiery zeal was again balked by the timidity and retreat of Montecuccoli's successor, Bournonville.

Meanwhile Louis XIV had bribed the Swedes with French gold to make a diversion in his favor by a Swedish invasion of Brandenburg. Gathering his troops together, Frederick William suddenly dashed back to the Elbe to protect his people. Pushing forward his cavalry under the Prince von Homburg, he caught the surprised Swedes on June 28, 1675, at Fehrbellin and won a decisive victory with some 6000 men against 8000. It was after this that he was hailed as the "Great" Elector, and the victory was later celebrated (with much poetic license) in Kleist's stirring drama, *Der Prinz von Homburg*. After Fehrbellin the Great Elector easily cleared the Swedes out of Brandenburg. In the course of the next three years he successfully besieged and stormed the fortresses of Stettin, Stralsund, and Greifswald, and conquered Swedish Pomerania.

In the winter of 1678–1679 Louis XIV encouraged the Swedes to ship an army of 16,000 across the Baltic to invade Prussia from the northeast, but the Great Elector annihilated it by despatching a force that was marched or transported in sledges over the frozen lagoons of the Kurisches and Frisches Haff. By these victories he hoped at last to realize his claim to the whole of Pomerania, which he had not been able to make good at the Peace of Westphalia. He was doomed, however, to the bitterest disappointment. While he had been fighting the Swedish-French alliance on the shores of the Baltic, his allies had tired of the fight on the Rhine and signed the Treaty of Nymwegen giving to France Franche-Comté and other territories belonging to the Holy Roman Empire. Louis XIV, who had occupied Cleves, was then in a position to use his great power to demand that Western Pomerania should be restored to Sweden.

Deserted by all his allies and faced with a French threat to keep Cleves, Frederick William was forced to accept on June 29, 1679, just four years after his brilliant victory of Fehrbellin, the Peace of St. Germain: he regained possession of Cleves, but he had to give back to Sweden all his hard-won conquests in Swedish Pomerania except a little strip of land on the right bank of the Oder opposite Stettin. His indignation turned against the Hapsburgs and the Dutch who had left him in the lurch, rather than against the French who sought to soften his disappointment over Pomerania by giving him some compensation in cash. During the next six years, therefore, he allied with the French and received their subsidies. Only when Louis's seizure of Strasbourg foreshadowed further aggressions against Germany, and when his persecution of the Calvinists reached a climax in the revocation of the Edict of Nantes in 1685, did the Great Elector return to his normal policy of defending the Empire and the Anglo-Dutch Protestant cause against the Catholic monarch of Versailles. The last password that he issued for the guard at Potsdam the day before his death on May 9, 1688, was significant: "Amsterdam and London!"

Military Revenues and Administration

During the Northern War the Great Elector had raised his army from 4000 to an efficient force of 27,000, not including 4000 men serving in garrisons. After 1660 he decided upon the policy of maintaining in time of peace, as a *standing army,* about half the force that he had raised by necessity in time of war as a fighting army. With characteristic thrift he found means of turning his standing army to profitable uses. Soldiers were employed in digging the famous Frederick William Canal connecting the Elbe and the Oder, thus making Berlin the center of water transportation between central Europe and Hamburg. Soldiers were conveniently used in transforming the Tiergarten area (now in the heart of modern Berlin) into a pleasant park and suburb and connecting it with Berlin by a broad avenue planted with linden trees that became celebrated among travelers as "Unter den Linden." In the war with France and Sweden the army was again increased to a fighting force of 45,000 in 1678, but with the return of peace, as in 1660, was again reduced by somewhat more than one-half, making a considerable standing army of about 18,000. This remained its average size until Louis XIV's invasion of the Palatinate in 1686, when it was increased again to 30,000. It made Brandenburg-Prussia, next to Austria, the strongest power in Germany and a highly prized ally in later wars.

The indirect effects of the standing army on internal administration were perhaps even more important than its direct effects on foreign policy in self-defense and new conquests. As the army was one of the first institutions that embodies the unity and efficiency of the whole Brandenburg-Prussian state, in contrast with the weakness and parochial attitude of the separate territories, so the organs of financial administration that were developed for the army's support soon came to form a centralized and efficient civil service. This gradually supplanted the various lax and decentralized agencies that had been managed by the Estates. By the time of the Great Elector's death, his absolutist officials had pretty generally taken the place of the particularistic agents of the Estates. So the two main pillars of the Prussian state arose side by side: the standing army and the civil service. This is a complicated subject, but a simplified statement of it, with the aid of the table at the end of the volume, will make clear its more important features, and will also indicate how local Brandenburg institutions (shown by dotted lines in the table) were extended to the Elector's other lands and were thus transformed into general organs (shown by solid lines) of the whole Brandenburg-Prussian state *(Gesammtstaat)*. It is essential for any student of Prussian history to have a clear grasp of the administrative apparatus which provided the foundations of Prussia's greatness.

Until the Northern War the troops in the Elector's various lands had stood under separate commands and never been united in a single army. As a first step toward centralization Freiherr von Sparr was given authority in 1651 over all the garrison troops except those in Brandenburg and Prussia; then in 1655 he was given general command over *all* the troops. If the Great Elector took over the command personally, as at the Battle of Warsaw and on many other campaigns, Sparr acted as his Chief of Staff. By the time of his death in 1688 Sparr had formed a group of officers into a permanent General Staff *(Generalstab)*.

Under Sparr's formal authority, but virtually independent of him, was the far more important General Commissariat. This was an extension of the system of War Commissars who had received and dispensed the new military tax *(Kontribution)* collected during the Thirty Years' War as already noted. In the Electorate and in each of the other territories a single Chief Commissar *(Ober-*

kriegskommissar) had been given authority over the District Commissars. In 1655 General Platen, a very able man who spoke several languages and had been on many missions, as well as having served as District Commissar in Priegnitz and as Privy Councilor since 1651, was appointed General Commissar for the whole state. He and his successors built up a well-organized General Commissariat (*Generalkommissariat*) for overseeing the collection and dispensing of the *Kontribution* from *all* the Great Elector's lands. The collection of this tax had at first been in the hands of the agents of the Estates, but as their power was undermined, the collection was taken over, in most of the territories by 1688, by the General Commissar's subordinates: the Chief Commissar in each province and by their subofficials, the District Commissars (*Kreiskommissare* in the rural districts, *Steuerkommissare* in the towns and *Aemterkommissare* on the Elector's domain lands).

The General Commissariat also saw to the recruiting, provisioning, and quartering of the army. It looked after the military hospitals, the care of invalid soldiers, and the exercise of military justice. Like a modern war department, it had charge of everything relating to the army except questions of strategy and leadership in the field that belonged to the General Staff. Its most important function, however, was to increase the military revenue and find other fruitful sources besides the *Kontribution*. It devised the productive graduated poll taxes of 1677–1679 during the Swedish-French War, in which the 250 gradations, covering every individual from "Our most gracious Master" at 1000 talers to postilions, poor artisans and peasants at one taler each, read like a fascinating social register. It formed a number of boards that were to tap or create taxable wealth: a *Commerzcollegium* to stimulate commerce and afford merchants speedy justice; a Stamp-tax Chest (*Stempelkasse*) to collect the revenue from the sale of the specially stamped paper required for legal documents; a so-called French Commissariat to bring in and settle the industrially valuable Huguenot refugees; and a Navy Chest (*Marinekasse* or *Chargenkasse*) to collect a tax from all public officials (with the kindly exception of clergy and school teachers) of one-half the first year's salary—a tax similar to the ecclesiastical "first fruits"—used originally toward creating a tiny navy but soon applied to the army. In its management of the grain stores and its other economic, political, and police activities the General Commissariat was a powerful factor in introducing mercantilism and prosperity by compulsion.

In 1652 the military correspondence, which had hitherto been handled for the Privy Council by the Elector's Privy Chancery, was delegated to a War Secretary under whom there developed in 1657 a Privy War Chancery (*Geheime Kriegskanzlei*). This issued the commissions for newly appointed officers, carried on the military correspondence, and kept the general records relating to the army. It worked in two rooms over the kitchen in the Berlin Schloss for a century—until in 1745 its paper records, unfortunately for the historian, were used by Frederick the Great to make wadding for cartridges! Besides this body, Sparr and Platen also had for their respective organizations special chanceries (*Feldmarschallskanzlei* and *Kommissariatskanzlei*).

After Schwartzenberg's military fiasco, the keeping and accounting of the meager Brandenburg military revenues, consisting mainly of the *Kontribution*, the bushel tax on grain, and certain war tolls, were done by their respective treasuries or chests (*Kontributionskasse, Metzkasse,* and *Lizentenkasse*), which in 1651 were merged into the War Chest (*Kriegskasse*). This continued till the end of the century primarily as a provincial Brandenburg receptacle, though it also received some revenues from the other provinces and was to that extent a general or central institution. During the Northern War, in order to provide cash on the spot for the needs of the marching army, there was created a Field War Chest (*Feldkriegskasse*). This sucked money from all the provinces, and after 1674 was enriched by the foreign subsidies and kept an invaluable account book which has been preserved.

Civil Revenues and Administration

In seventeenth century Brandenburg, unlike modern states, civil and military revenues were wholly different and distinct from one another. The latter, though of more recent origin, were soon larger in amount and more important in the proliferation of centralizing institutions in the growing absolutist state. The civil revenues, to use a modern term, or, more properly, the patrimonial income of the prince, originated in the Middle Ages and in the Great Elector's day were still of a primitive and semi-feudal character. They were chiefly of two sorts: (1) the domain revenues managed by the Comptroller's Office (*Amtskammer*) and consisting of money rent and of "payments in kind," such as grain, cattle, dairy produce, and firewood, from the surplus product of the manorial lands that the Electors kept and had cultivated for their own needs; and (2) the "regalian rights," consisting of the profits of justice; fines, tolls on roads and rivers and harbors, a beer tax, a tax on Jews; and profits from coinage and from various commercial monopolies like the salt, postal, glass, iron, copper, and millstone administrations. The regalian revenues were paid partly into the Exchequer (*Hofrentei*) and partly into the Privy Purse (*Chatulle*).

All the civil revenues were frightfully depleted by the terrible ravages and general economic desolation of the Thirty Years' War. In Brandenburg more than half of the population and cattle had disappeared and nearly half of the tillable land had become "waste." In the administration of the Elector's domain lands the stewards kept no proper accounts and often kept for themselves what they should have turned in at Berlin. As about five-sixths of the domain revenues were in the form of natural products which were not evaluated in cash equivalents, and as all officials received the greater part of their salaries from these natural products instead of in cash, no one had any notion of the total amount and value of the domain revenues or cost of the Elector's household and administration. Many of the domains had been mortgaged during the long war and so either produced nothing or were a positive burden. Even those which the Electors had managed to retain were burdened by their convenient but careless habit of making gifts or payments by "assignments" upon this or that domain revenue—sometimes when no such revenue actually existed; worse still, no accounting was made of these prodigal assignments.

The Great Elector, well aware of the financial evils, sought to remedy them soon after the war was over. In 1651 he appointed a commission of four of his ablest advisors with the significant new title of State Treasury Councilors (*Staatskammerräte*) to reform the manage‹ ment of the domains in all his lands. Unfortunately, they were so occupied with their other duties as active Privy Councilors and other matters, and then with the Northern War, that they accomplished virtually nothing. Nor did the individual men (Canstein, Grumbkow, Jena, Gladebeck, and Meinders) who followed them from 1659 to 1683 do much better, except that in 1673 there was established a Court State Chest (*Hofstaatskasse*). This new treasury (making three) with the *Chatulle* and *Hofrentei*) was created to assure a larger and more regular income for the Elector's expanding household and state administration. It was therefore provided with a certain fairly fixed income from various domains and from the local exchequers of *all* the Elector's lands. Until 1674 some of these revenues from Prussia, Cleves, and elsewhere had been paid into the two Brandenburg treasuries, the *Chatulle* and *Hofrentei*, which to a certain extent had therefore been *general* treasuries for the Brandenburg-Prussian state. After the establishment of the *Hofstaatskasse*, however, the *Hofrentei* sank back again into a provincial Brandenburg exchequer and therefore came to be known as a *Landrentei*.

In 1683 an East Frisian Baron, Dodo zu Knyphausen, whose great ability was equaled by his great modesty, entered Frederick William's service. He at last accomplished revolutionary reforms in the administration of the domains and greatly increased the revenues from them. He gradually redeemed the manorial estates that had been mortgaged. He let out the domains on short leases (*Arrende* or *Pächte*) so that he was sure of fixed rents instead of trusting to the doubtful honesty of managing stewards. He translated all "payments in kind" into cash equivalents. He required strict quarterly accountings of all "assignments" as well as of all domain cash-rents and produce and of all household and other administrative payments. He was thus able in 1689 to draw up for the first time a systematic budget (*General Etat*) of all the Elector's civil revenues and expenditures from all his lands. It showed a handsome civil cash revenue of 1,533,000 talers, as compared with a meager 297,000 in 1664 and a pitiful 59,000 in 1644. To assist him, Knyphausen also organized a board (*collegium*) of technical experts known in 1689 as the Privy Comptroller's Office (*Geheime Hofkammer*).

Prosperity by Compulsion

Besides developing these various means for extracting larger military and civil revenues, the Great Elector took innumerable measures for increasing the population, prosperity, and productivity of his lands, thus lessening the financial burden upon the individual.

In 1649 he settled seventy Frisian families, well acquainted with the better agricultural methods of the Dutch, in Brandenburg. A generation later he brought in eighty Swiss families. With characteristic toleration he admitted Jews from Poland who paid annual tribute money for protection against prevailing hatred and prejudice and who had to promise not to charge usurious rates of interest or deal in stolen goods. Most valuable were the 20,000 refugee French Huguenots whom Frederick William aided to settle by sending them guides and traveling money and by giving them land, building material, exemption from taxes for six years, and many other privileges. They formed at one time a sixth of the population of Berlin, with a church and a school conducted in French, and helped immeasurably to raise the city's economic and cultural level by their new industries and quick intelligence. They enriched the Electoral dinner table by popularizing the eating of lettuce, asparagus, cauliflowers, and artichokes. From their numbers were formed a cavalry regiment under Baron Briquemault and an infantry regiment under the Marquis de Varenne. Two companies of young French nobles, the *Grands Mousquetaires,* gorgeous in red coats, gold braid and white-feathered hats, served as a kind of officers' training school from whose descendants came many distinguished Prussian officers.

For a century and a half the Counts of Thurn and Taxis had enjoyed an imperial monopoly for their postal system throughout Germany, with many offices in foreign cities. To take its place in his own lands and save its charges, the Great Elector established in 1662 a postal system of his own. It carried at first only official dispatches, then letters and packages for others, and finally coach passengers. With Berlin as the center of the postal network, it aided the process of centralization of government by putting the central boards in quick touch with the local ones. The post went twice a week from Königsberg through Berlin to Cleves in what was considered in those days as the incredibly quick time of one week. The postal system was also agreeably remunerative, its profits showing a uniformly upward curve from 17,000 talers in 1662 to 80,000 in 1688.

The purchase and sale of salt from Lüneburg or Hamburg was also exploited by the Great Elector as a profitable government monopoly (without the abuses of the French *gabelle*), and averaged a return of more than 40,000 talers a year from 1662 to 1680. After 1680, when the acquisition of the Magdeburg lands gave him possession of a salt supply of his own (the Stassfurt and Halle deposits that are among the richest salt beds in Europe), the salt monopoly became much more productive until it was finally abolished in 1867. The millstone monopoly brought in a small but steady revenue, but the efforts for the state exploitation of iron, copper, glass, and some other manufactures were financial failures.

For the promotion of agriculture the Great Elector ran a botanical garden and experimental station in front of the Berlin Palace for trying out foreign trees and plants of all sorts as to suitability for his sandy lands. The Oranienburg estate, named after his first wife, where Dutch methods were employed, was also a model farm for all his subjects. To promote the planting of fruit trees he decreed that no bridegroom on his domains might marry until he had first planted at least six new trees.

By the application of his native common sense and by the trial-and-error method, rather than by mere copying of Dutch and French mercantilist notions, Frederick William rigorously supervised the gilds and controlled exports and imports after the mercantilist fashion in the interests of his people as a whole. In his efforts to create a navy and found colonies, however, he was two centuries ahead of his time; he and his successors soon found that their resources were still too small to compete successfully with the ruthless colonial and naval power of the Dutch, the French, and the English. So his successors wisely confined their main efforts to strengthening their power on the continent of Europe.

C H A P T E R . . . 3

The Development
of the Prussian State
(1688–1786)

It was a curious trait of the Hohenzollern dynasty that the heir was usually a contrast to the ruling prince. This often caused unedifying family discord, for the father could not understand the son and the son could not appreciate the good qualities of the father. For the Prussian state, however, this family trait was not wholly unfortunate, but rather the reverse, for the son supplied qualities that were lacking in the father but that were valuable for the state. The Great Elector's son Frederick (1688–1713) lacked the solid financial understanding and practical administrative sense of the Great Elector, but his passion for pomp and dignity and his love of the arts led him to elevate himself to the rank of king, and his capital, Berlin, to a center of correspondingly greater splendor and culture. His son Frederick William I (1713–1740) more like the Great Elector, resumed the crucial task of increasing his income and his army, but cared little for music, philosophy, or literature. These, however, were precisely the subjects that most interested the next heir, Crown Prince Fritz, a fact that caused a most distressing domestic conflict between father and son. Fortunately, when Fritz became King as Frederick II in 1740, he had developed into such a many-sided genius that he was able to continue his youthful cultural interests, and at the same time rival his father in continuing the task of building up the army, the finances, and the administrative structure of the state. Moreover, whereas Frederick William I had generally avoided war because he could not bear to see his beloved battalions decimated in battle, Frederick the Great used the army to acquire new lands and power for his country and greatly increased prestige for himself as its king.

Frederick I (1688–1713)

Frederick, the third Brandenburg Elector of that name, inherited the improved financial and military machinery and the able officials of the Great Elector. Consequently the revenues continued to rise for nine years; his credit was so good that he was able to borrow heavily and there seemed to be plenty of money for his lavish expenditures. He joined at once with the armies of the Emperor and of William of Orange, in return for the promise of considerable subsidies, and helped drive the French out of Germany and the Netherlands. At the Peace of Ryswick, however, in 1697, he felt that his dignity was injured by the scant consideration with which he was treated by his allies and was indignant that he was rewarded with no territory. The blame for this he unjustly laid on his chief minister, Eberhard von Danckelman.

This remarkable man, who came from a Calvinist family in Münster, had been Prince Frederick's tutor, and for years enjoyed the Elector's absolute confidence and favor. Danckelman and his six brothers were appointed to numerous lucrative offices. Danckelman himself was given almost undisturbed control of the government. By 1697, however, he had aroused the envy of the nobles and other officials by his power and wealth. He had also aroused the enmity of the Electress, Sophie Charlotte, by his close hold over the purse strings and by an exclusive influence over her husband that she coveted for herself. Court intrigues that sought to poison the Elector's mind against his all powerful minister triumphed when Frederick convinced himself that Danckelman was to blame for humiliations at Ryswick, and especially when he found that Danckelman was opposed to his pet project of making himself King of Prussia. Danckelman feared the kingship would be opposed by the Emperor and other princes, and in any case would entail too expensive a royal court. On December 4, 1697, the all powerful minister was suddenly dismissed from all his offices and soon brought to trial on unsubstantiated charges of corruption. The ungrateful king confiscated all his property and kept him in prison until 1707 after the death of Sophie Charlotte.

Frederick's desire for the kingship was whetted by seeing his neighbors raised in rank: the Duke of Brunswick was elevated to be Elector of Hanover in 1692, and his son already had the prospect of becoming George I of England; and the Elector of Saxony abandoned Lutheranism to become King of Poland in 1697. Frederick's opportunity came with the death of poor Carlos II of Spain on November 1, 1700; the Emperor was willing to buy the support of 8000 Brandenburg troops to secure his claim to the Spanish succession by agreeing to recognize the royal title whenever Frederick should proclaim himself king in Prussia. Once the Emperor's consent was gained, Frederick lost no time. On January 18, 1701, in the presence of the Prussian Estates assembled for the purpose, he placed a crown upon his own head and another upon that of his wife. To emphasize his independence of the church, the coronation took place in the Königsberg castle; only after-

wards did the royal procession then move to a chapel
where the king and queen were consecrated by two Protestant bishops specially created for the occasion. To emphasize his position as sovereign prince outside the Empire
and to avoid complications with Poland which ruled West
Prussia, Frederick took the title King *in* Prussia (*Rex in
Borussia*). At the same time, using the emblem of the old
Teutonic Knights, he founded the distinguished Order of
the Black Eagle, with their motto indicating just reward
and punishment: *Suum cuique.* To regard the coronation
as a mere act of vanity on Frederick's part would be a
mistake. In an age when formalities counted for much, it
marked a very real increase in the power and prestige of
the Brandenburg-Prussian state, and gave it the rank in
Europe to which the Great Elector's solid achievements
entitled it. Though only king "in Prussia," Elector Frederick III was soon known as Frederick I, King of Prussia;
people spoke of the "Royal Prussian Army"; and the administration in all his provinces was henceforth known as
the "Royal Prussian Administration." The crown became
a new symbol of unity.

Frederick also secured from the Emperor the privilege of
having lawsuits involving less than 2500 gulden exempted
from appeal to the imperial courts. This did not apply to
the Electorate of Brandenburg which by the Golden Bull
of 1356 had long enjoyed a complete *privilegio de non
appellando,* nor to East Prussia which lay outside the Holy
Roman Empire. These two lands (and also Ravensberg)
continued to have their local supreme courts (in Brandenburg the *Kammergericht*). For all his other lands
Frederick I established in 1703 a new High Court of
Appeal (*Ober-Appellationsgericht*) as a step toward the
centralization of justice. By a further step in 1748, as a
result of the reforms toward legal simplicity and uniformity of the great jurist Cocceji, this court, commonly
known as the High Tribunal (*Ober-Tribunal*), became a

court of appeal for Brandenburg and Ravensberg as well as for the other provinces (except Prussia).

The Great Elector had done much for the improvement of Berlin, protecting it with defensive fortifications, providing fire protection and street lighting, laying out the Unter den Linden avenue and the Friedrich and Dorotheen settlements on either side of it, and establishing in his palace the valuable public library with rare oriental manuscripts. It was to become as the Prussian State Library one of the half dozen greatest libraries of the world. Frederick I was ambitious to do much more. He enlarged the palace and built the massive arsenal *(Zeughaus),* two architectural masterpieces destroyed by fighting in 1945. He added seven churches to his capital. He imported Dutch and French engineers, architects, painters, and musicians, but none of them left such a lasting mark on the baroque style of the period as his own famous architect and sculptor Andreas Schlüter.

Frederick's wife Sophie Charlotte of Hanover was a great help to him in making Berlin a cultural center. With unusual personal charm and with an interest in literature and philosophy which, however, was more lively than profound, she attracted to her court many notable men. Among them was the versatile genius Leibniz, famous as theologian, historian, philosopher, and statesman, as well as for the discovery of calculus. He was made first president of the new Berlin Academy of Sciences, established in 1701, which combined in its aims the scientific interests of the Royal Society in London and the French Academy at Paris. For its endowment it was given a monopoly of the manufacture and sale of calendars, which happened at the moment to be rather lucrative as Frederick I had just dropped out eleven days and adopted the "new style" of Pope Gregory XIII. This new Gregorian calendar, now in universal use throughout Christendom, had been dutifully accepted by most Roman Catholic countries in 1582, but foolishly rejected by most Protestant rulers for a half a century or so longer. The Berlin Academy suffered a blight under the unsympathetic austerity of Frederick William I, but under the patronage of Frederick the Great began to live up to the high hopes of its founder, and in the nineteenth century became one of the world's most distinguished learned societies. Sophie Charlotte's name is perpetuated in Charlottenburg, where Frederick I built another palace and where there gradually grew a pleasant residential suburb to the west of Berlin beyond the Great Elector's Tiergarten.

The University of Halle, dedicated in 1694 and provided with funds from the exploitation of the rich, newly-acquired salt deposits nearby, together with the earlier universities at Frankfort on the Oder (1506), at Königsberg (1544), and at Duisburg in the Rhineland (1655), gave Frederick a seat of learning in each of his principal provinces. Halle soon became doubly distinguished for its progressive jurisprudence and its tolerant and practical theology in contrast to the narrow scholasticism and dogmatic Lutheranism or Calvinism of most of the German universities. Here Christian Thomasius (1655–1728) had the courage to defy tradition by lecturing in German instead of in Latin. He was a pioneer in restoring the German language as a medium for scholars, gave a stimulus to the study of Germanic law in contrast to prevailing Roman law, and edited in German a legal magazine. He attacked witchcraft trials and the use of torture, favored the theories of natural law already developed by Grotius and Pufendorf, and prepared the way for the enlightened despotism of the eighteenth century. A. H. Francke (1663–1727), besides teaching the new, lovable, Quaker-like Christianity known as Pietism which was being preached at Berlin by P. J. Spener (1635–1703), aroused an interest in popular education in his orphan asylum at

Halle, and corresponded with Cotton Mather at Harvard College. So from Halle came pastors, jurists, and civil servants, trained with a progressive outlook in government and a broad toleration in religion, who were of decisive advantage to the new Prussian monarchy.

The War of the Spanish Succession (1701–1713), and the Second Northern War (1700–1721)

The fall of Danckelman in 1697 involved that of Knyphausen and many other able officials, and opened the way to dishonest favorites who wheedled Frederick I by flattery and by finding money for his royal court and the embellishment of Berlin. These favorites, Wartenberg, Wartensleben, and Wittgenstein, later execrated as "the three W[oes]," mismanaged the numerous offices which they assumed, enriched themselves, and piled up a state debt. The household expenditure rose from quarter of a million talers in 1687 to nearly half a million in 1711. Foreign war and the pest and famine which swept over Europe in 1709 and the following years finally revealed the mismanagement and dishonesty of the king's incompetent ministers. An investigation, largely instituted by Crown Prince Frederick William, led to their downfall in 1711 and to reforms that became drastic as soon as Frederick William became king in 1713.

Meanwhile Prussia had been caught between two great wars. In the east the accession of the ambitious Charles XII of Sweden and his defeat of Peter the Great at Narva in 1700 opened the Second Northern War; he then turned back to conquer Poland and set up his camp in Saxony near the Prussian frontier. In the west the death of

Carlos II and the rival claims of the French, Hapsburgs, and Bavarians to his inheritance opened the War of the Spanish Succession; Dutch and English took a decisive part in this war when Louis XIV foolishly recognized the Stuart Pretender as King of England as a deathbed gesture to the deposed James II. What should Frederick I do?

Since Prussia's resources did not allow him to divide his efforts by intervening in both conflicts, Frederick had to choose. His true interests lay in the east where, by taking the side of the rising power of Russia, he had the prospect of acquiring Polish (or West) Prussia and Swedish Pomerania and of winning a strong position on the Baltic. But neither Charles XII nor Peter the Great were willing to pay the subsidies on which the Prussian army was more than ever dependent, owing to the financial mismanagement of Danckelman's successors. On the other hand, by taking up arms against Louis XIV, Frederick would fulfill his coronation agreement with the Emperor and continue the Great Elector's policy of protecting Germany and Protestant interests. Furthermore, he would probably promote his claims to the Orange family lands, and he felt that there was always safety in subsidies. So he chose the west, and on December 30, 1701, joined the Grand Alliance against Louis XIV.

In the War of the Spanish Succession Prussian "auxiliary forces" fought with distinction all over Europe—at Blenheim on the Danube under Marlborough, in Italy, on the Rhine, and in the Netherlands. At the Peace of Utrecht in 1713 Prussia acquired some bits of the Orange inheritance which Frederick I had annexed during the war: Mörs and Lingen in 1702, and Tecklenburg in 1707, near Cleves; Neuchâtel on the western border of Switzerland in 1707; and Upper Gelders in the Spanish Netherlands in 1713, as compensation for parts of the Orange inheritance which went to France.

Frederick I, engraving.
(New York Public Library, Picture Collection)

Frederick William I, engraving. *(Giraudon)*

In the Northern War Charles XII, drawn far from home into the depths of southern Russia, was defeated at Poltava in 1709 and fled to Turkey where he lived in helpless exile for five years. Meanwhile Russians and Poles invaded Swedish Pomerania, disregarding the neutrality of the Empire. Frederick I, with his troops in the west, could do nothing to defend Germany's eastern frontier. After his death on February 25, 1713, a few weeks before the Treaty of Utrecht was signed on April 11, his successor Frederick William I, received a visit from Peter the Great in Berlin. Peter urged him to join in besieging the fortresses in Swedish Pomerania, but the King replied that he needed a year to put his army and finances in order. In October Peter bombarded and captured Stettin. As a gesture of respect for the neutrality of the Empire he agreed that Frederick William should hold Stettin in sequestration, pay the Russians 400,000 talers for war costs, and maintain the neutrality of Pomerania for the remainder of the Northern War. In 1714 this arrangement was suddenly upset by Charles XII. Dashing on horseback from Turkey to the Baltic, he threw himself into the Pomeranian fortress of Stralsund, and threatened Peter, Frederick William, and the neighboring German princes. Then at last Prussia took up arms. In alliance with the Danes she conquered Stralsund, Rügen, and Wismar, while George I of England and Hanover seized the secularized bishoprics of Bremen and Verden which Sweden had held since the Thirty Years' War. After Charles XII had been killed in an attack on Denmark, the Northern War was gradually brought to a close by a series of treaties between 1719 and 1721. Frederick William I, by the Treaty of Stockholm (February 1, 1720), retained Stettin which he had held in sequestration for six years, acquired the eastern half of Swedish Pomerania stretching from the Oder to the Peene, and paid Sweden two million talers for it. Prussia now controlled both banks of the lower Oder and possessed in Stettin a first-class Baltic port.

Frederick William I (1713–1740)

Born in 1688, Frederick William was brought up by a French nurse, a French tutor, and a Prussian noble of French ancestry, Count Alexander von Dohna. From these excellent people he learned to speak French as a mother tongue, but when he wrote it or Germanized it in the barbarous habit of the day he exercised a sovereign contempt for grammar and spelling. His German was coarse but vigorous. His innumerable royal comments on state papers, expressed phonetically, brutally, humorously, and vehemently, stamp him as one of the most interesting, forceful, hard-headed and misunderstood of Hohenzollern rulers.

From his tutors also he received a Calvinistic reverence for God Almighty's power and a puritanic temper. This made him abhor the loose life and cabals of his father's court, and inspired his own reign with a sense of public duty as powerful as Kant's categorical imperative. He hated all shams, deceit, intrigues, and costly display (except in military matters), and was himself so naïvely free from these faults that he was sometimes taken in by others. He had by nature a violent temper that made him bring his cane down unmercifully upon his family and his subjects.

The king worked very strenuously himself and expected his civil servants to do likewise, "for I pay them to work"—though he did not pay them much; *travailler pour le Roi de Prusse* became proverbial for hard work and small pay. He was, however, at bottom genuinely kind-hearted and solicitous for the well-being of his people. If he struck loiterers, grafters, and people who got in his way or opposed him, he at the same time provided for poor widows, maintained a great orphan asylum at Potsdam, and continually warned lawyers and domain officers not to plague the people with long vexatious suits and unjust exactions. He was quick to scold and condemn, but also ready to pardon—especially if the offender happened to be one of his beloved soldiers. A musketeer who had stolen 6000 talers was sentenced by a judge to the usual penalty of the gallows; his colonel who did not want to lose a good fighter appealed to the king; Frederick William summoned the judge, knocked out a couple of his teeth with the ever-ready cane, and the musketeer went scot free.

Already as crown prince, Frederick William manifested the twin interests that were to characterize his reign: rigid economy and an imposing army. From his allowance, of which he kept a precise "reckoning of my ducats," he saved 50,000 talers, besides making generous church donations and building his favorite hunting lodge at Wusterhausen. Here he made an excellent collection of military weapons of all sorts, and trained and equipped at his own expense a militia company of "big fellows." In 1709 he joined the Prussian troops in the War of the Spanish Succession, fought under the eye of Marlborough, was allowed to recommend officers for promotion and formed an intimate friendship with his father's ablest general, Field-Marshal Leopold von Dessau ("the Old Dessauer").

For a full quarter of a century, 1688–1713, from the cradle to the throne, the growing heir had seen his country involved in almost continuous war. To his chagrin he realized that Prussia's army, and consequently her whole foreign policy, was dependent on foreign subsidies. He resolved to make himself independent of subsidies, to build up a war treasure of his own, and to have an army large enough to defend Prussia and to follow a policy in accordance with her own true interests. This was a policy of peace. With the brief exception of the tail end of the Northern War, Frederick William kept his country out of war. At his accession in 1713 he inherited a bankrupt administration and an army of 40,000 men. At his death in 1740 he left his son a model administration in which the annual domain revenue had risen from 1,300,000 to 3,300,000 talers, a war treasure of 8,000,000, and an army of 83,000, regarded as the most efficient and best disciplined in Europe. How did he do it?

Administrative and Financial Reforms

More than two years before his accession Frederick William had worked actively to get rid of some of the worst abuses of the cabal administration of "the three Woes." It was largely owing to him that committees of investigation were appointed in 1710. Their reports, in spite of the efforts of the ministers to suppress or belittle them, led to the downfall of Wartenberg, Wartensleben, and Wittgenstein. With their removal, the supervision and keeping of all the domain and regalian revenues was placed under a single able man, Ernst von Kameke, who had the full confidence of the crown prince. This consolidation of the civil revenue administration was completed as soon as he became king by the organization of a General Finance Directory and a General Finance Chest. The former (*Generalfinanzdirectorium*) took the place of the old *Hofkammer* created by Knyphausen and described above in Chapter 2. The latter (*Generalfinanzkasse*) swallowed up the *Chatulle* which disappeared, and also the *general* revenues of the *Hofrentei* which sank back into a provincial Brandenburg *Landrentei*. The *Hofstaatskasse,* instead of continuing to receive a fixed revenue for the household, survived as a mere accounting institution for it.

Frederick I's cabal ministers, before their removal from office, had sought to raise ready cash by mortgaging the domains or by granting them out on hereditary leases, so that the domains were in danger of being virtually lost as a royal possession. This was stopped at once in 1711. Instead, there was a return to the Knyphausen system of leasing for a short term—usually six years, so that if the domains increased in value a higher rent might be charged when the lease was renewed. By these and other reforms, and by Kameke's strict and honest supervision, the domain revenues were almost doubled between 1711 and 1713.

Besides increasing the civil revenues, Fredrick William I cut down drastically the civil expenditures so that the surplus might be used for the army. With filial piety he gave his father a gorgeous funeral such as he knew would have delighted Frederick I. Berlin saw its pomp and pageantry for the last time. Then, recognizing that Prussia was too poor to be both Athens and Sparta, the new king chose Sparta. Sending for the long list of court officials, he drew his pen through two-thirds of the names. Some of those dismissed were at once given places in the army. Those who remained had their salaries reduced to make them realize that he was now undisputed master and that if they were to have a raise again they must earn it by diligence and devotion. Thus the cost of the household and administration was cut down by three-fourths—from 421,000 talers in 1711 to 102,000 in 1713. When he went to Königsberg to receive the homage of the East Prussian Estates, he covered the distance in four days with a modest retinue of 50 horses and spent 2547 talers. When his father had gone there for his coronation in 1701, he took fourteen days with a train of 2000 horses and spent 5 million talers.

The ranking of the officials who were spared by Frederick William's pen was altered in accordance with his preference for soldiers over civilians. The gradations in rank, which had risen from 32 in 1688 to 142, were cut to 46. The High Chamberlain and the Grand Master of the Wardrobe at the head of the list disappeared altogether and were replaced by the Field-Marshal and generals;

Privy Councilors were moved down from 5th to 6th place; and major generals were advanced from 19th to 9th, colonels from 43rd to 19th, and lieutenant colonels from 67th to 33rd, and so on. As the King said: "50,000 soldiers are worth more than 100,000 ministers."

All officials were to be inspired with a holy fear of the king's authority and with his sense of military devotion, discipline, and punctuality. The Saxon Minister at Berlin, Manteuffel, reported:

Every day His Majesty gives new proofs of his justice. Walking recently at Potsdam at six in the morning, he saw a post-coach arrive with several passengers who knocked for a long time at the post-house which was still closed. The King, seeing that no one opened the door, joined them in knocking and even knocked in some window-panes. The master of the post then opened the door and scolded the travelers, for no one recognized the King. But His Majesty let himself be known by giving the official some good blows of his cane and drove him from his house and his job after apologizing to the travelers for his laziness. Examples of this sort, of which I could relate several others, make everybody alert and exact.

The military revenues were also increased. In East Prussia a new general land tax (*Generalhufenschoss*) brought in a great deal more than the Great Elector's land tax. It was also more equitable, because it was now for the first time levied upon the land of the nobles as well as upon that of the peasants. The excise was made fairly uniform throughout the kingdom, and, with the growing well-being of the people, rapidly augmented and even exceeded the land tax. It was also used as a mercantilist measure for protecting and fostering Prussia's own manufactures at a time when the boundaries of the state were too irregular and extended to permit of an effective tariff frontier. Nobles who still held their land on feudal tenure were given their land in fee simple on payment of 40 talers; this commuted the military knights' service for which they were still theoretically liable, but which had no place in the new Prussian army. Instead of serving their feudal overlord by fighting as in the Middle Ages, the nobles now served the Prussian state by paying—by helping to support the army in which so many of them were engaged as officers.

The administration of the military revenues, which had been developed by Platen and his successors, was put in charge of a board known as the General War Commissariat (*Generalkriegskommissariat*). Its president was Friedrich Wilhelm von Grumbkow, an able and active man, who until his death in 1739 was one of Frederick William's most influential ministers. It supervised the Provincial Commissariats, which in turn supervised the local military tax collectors (cf. p. 70). The latter, in their exercise of wide police power and of economic control in enforcing mercantilist measures, were active in stamping out the remnants of the provincial spirit of opposition of the Estates and in completing the work of establishing Prussian absolutism begun by the Great Elector.

The General Directory of 1723 and Cabinet Government

Frederick William found that the dual administration of the civil and military revenues gave rise to many painful conflicts between the General Finance Directory and the General War Commissariat, and especially between their respective subordinate officials. The domains officials represented primarily agrarian interests and wanted freedom of export for grain, wool, and lumber. The commissariat officials, on the other hand, were more concerned with fiscal, manufacturing, and restrictive mercantilist interests.

Both groups, in their zeal to satisfy Frederick William's desire for more revenues, tended to encroach upon each other. To put an end to this "confusion," the king retired to a hunting lodge for the Christmas season and worked out a long "instruction" that consolidated the hitherto separate civil and military revenue administrations under a single supreme board. This new body, established in January 1723, rejoiced in the clumsy but unambiguous name of General Supreme Finance War and Domains Directory (*General-Ober-Finanz-Kriegs-und Domänen-Directorium*), commonly called for short the General Directory. It comprised four departments whose heads were to report on their respective fields on certain days as follows:

1. Grumbkow (Mondays): Prussia, Pomerania; Frontiers and Agriculture.
2. Creutz (Wednesdays): Minden, Ravensberg; General Budget.
3. Krautt (Thursdays): Brandenburg, Magdeburg, Halberstadt; Army.
4. Goerne (Fridays): Cleves-Mark, Neuchâtel, Mörs, Gelders; Postal System and Coinage.

As is evident, the departments were partly regional and reminiscent of the territorial growth of Prussia, and partly functional like the departments of government in a modern state. Each department had no separate and distinct life of its own; it merely prepared the business assigned to it for consideration by the General Directory as a whole. Each of the four department ministers had three or four assistant colleagues who also sat and voted in the plenary session. Each minister presided in turn on the day he presented his business, and then reported the discussion and resulting decisions to the king for his approval.

Under Frederick the Great five more departments were added, all of which were functional and modern in character: a Department of Commerce and Industry (1740); of Army Supplies (1746) as a result of his experiences in the

First Silesian Wars; and, in his reconstruction work after the devastation of the Seven Years' War, the Departments of Excise and Tolls (1766), Mines (1768), and Forestry (1770). Though Frederick William I's successors somewhat undermined the authority of the General Directory by the growing tendency toward "cabinet government" and by the appointment of "immediate commissions" to deal with special questions directly under the orders of the king, the General Directory of 1723, with some modifications, remained for four-score years the supreme governing board of the Prussian Monarchy until the reforms of Stein after the disaster at Jena.

In similar fashion Frederick William I consolidated the provincial domains and commissariat administrations into single collegial boards. Their members were forbidden to be residents of the provinces in which they served. This provision, as in the case of Richelieu's intendants in France, aimed to prevent officials from favoring friends and relatives. It was, however, in flat contradiction with the loudly demanded "right of the native born" of earlier days, and was significant of the way the fresh breeze of royal absolutism was sweeping away the sultry particularism of the Estates.

The central treasuries for the civil and military revenues (*Generalfinanzkasse* and *Generalkriegskasse*) were still kept separate because of the king's fear that military revenues might be diverted away from the army to other objects, as had happened under Frederick I. Under Frederick William I all revenues flowed into these two central treasuries. Frederick the Great, however, after 1763 assigned certain ordinary sources of revenue to each of these treasuries; thereafter, all new sources of revenue, such as the revenues from Silesia and from his new French tariff, coffee and tobacco monopolies, and so forth, flowed into a new *Dispositionskasse*. This third treasury, as its name implies, was at the private disposition of the king; he

made expenditures from it without consulting his ministers—mainly expenditures for the army and for the
amelioration of agriculture and industry after the im-
poverishment of the Seven Years' War. The income of this
Dispositionskasse rose during the peaceful second half of
his reign to exceed that of both the old treasuries. This
system of uncontrolled personal royal expenditure worked
well enough under an exact, energetic, and shrewd administrator like Frederick the Great, but was disastrous
under his weak and spendthrift successor.

In order to get the basis for a general budget of all his
revenues and expenditures, Frederick William I set up in
1723 a Supreme Accounting Office (*Oberrechenkammer*).
It received and checked all the accounts. Its president was
Creutz, who also, as minister in charge of the Second
Department of the General Directory, prepared the general budget.

Frederick William had declared that he himself would
be President of the General Directory, in order to lend it
"more luster, authority, and impressiveness," but actually
he almost never attended its meetings; the always empty
presidential chair was merely the symbol of the supreme
centralized authority that resided in the king. One of the
reasons for this was that the General Directory sat in the
Berlin Schloss, while Frederick William usually lived at
Potsdam or at one of his hunting lodges. Another reason
was the growing tendency toward "cabinet" government
at the expense of the Privy Council.

The Privy Council, after being for a century the
supreme central board, had been gradually stripped of
much of its business that was handed over to special indi-
viduals, commissions, or boards. Under Frederick I it met
less frequently and was attended by only a few members;
nor did the king usually preside in it as had been the
Great Elector's regular habit when he was in Berlin. The
consideration of foreign affairs, which had been one of the

chief reasons for its foundation in 1604 and which for more than eighty years had formed one of its main items of discussion, was handed over after the fall of Danckelman to four Privy Councilors who formed a new *Staatskonferenz;* this was later sometimes known as the *Cabinetsministerium* and was the forerunner of the modern Ministry of Foreign Affairs. Legal petitions and appeals to the Elector as the supreme fountain of justice, which for half a century had been dealt with in the Privy Council, were handed over in 1658, during the stress of business of the First Northern War, to four newly created councilors who with the Vice-Chancellor formed henceforth a Judicial Committee of the Privy Council, later known as the *Justizrat.* Other general questions, aside from foreign affairs, legal matters, and finance, were occasionally dealt with in the eighteenth century by a small group of select Privy Councilors forming what came to be known as the Privy State Council (*Geheimer Staatsrat*).

Under Frederick William I, and still more under Frederick the Great, the king tended more and more to decide matters personally himself in his private apartment or "cabinet" and to issue orders by dictation to cabinet secretaries. The king no longer ruled *in* council but *from* the cabinet. This change became most marked under Frederick the Great whose residence at Sans Souci in Potsdam necessitated written communications with the administrative boards which sat in Berlin. This Prussian "cabinet government" (which of course had nothing in common with the English institution of the same name) marked the extreme form of centralization and absolutism, and made possible Frederick II's remarkable achievement as an enlightened despot. It worked well under such alert, intelligent, hard-working, and conscientious monarchs as Frederick William I and Frederick the Great, but was to prove disastrous under their immediate successors during the storms of the French Revolution and Napoleonic invasion.

The Army

Frederick William I has often been called "the royal drill sergeant." Certainly he gave a new spirit, discipline, and efficiency to the institution that he had most at heart. He began by purging the officer corps of unworthy men, many of whom were foreign adventurers. Their places were given to his own nobles, who were forbidden to hire themselves out to other princes, according to the common practice of the day. For the instruction of their sons he founded a cadet corps at Berlin. This military employment of his own nobles helped to strengthen the bond between the nobility and the army and to wipe out the remnants of the old local opposition to the absolutist instrument of the new monarchy. The Junker nobility, proud of their class and accustomed to command the peasants on their landed estates, quickly developed in the army a strong *esprit de corps* and a sense of duty, discipline, and social superiority that was thenceforth characteristic of the Prussian officer caste. They felt that the King, who after 1725 always wore a uniform, was one of their number.

The recruiting of the common soldiers lay, not with the higher military authorities, but in the hands of the captains who received a lump sum for enrolling and maintaining their companies. The recruiting officers often came into conflict with one another for men, and often used deceit or compulsion that led to protests, opposition, and violence, especially when they attempted to get recruits from the lands of Prussia's neighbors. To remedy these abuses Frederick William adopted in 1733 the canton system. The kingdom was divided into more or less equal districts or cantons, each of which was to supply the men for a particular regiment.

Soldiers were recruited mainly from the peasant class, served for a long period of years, and were therefore virtually a professional or mercenary army. The economic loss of withdrawing men from agriculture was much lessened by the king's provision that soldiers who had been once well drilled were released on furlough for nine months of the year; it lessened also the cost of maintenance and was naturally very welcome to the captains; only for short periods of spring and fall training were the companies brought up to their full numbers.

Frederick William I built some great barracks in Berlin and quartered many regiments in the various fortresses, but for the most part soldiers were lodged with families in the garrison towns. They either paid for their board or bought and prepared their own food, or had it done by their wives who frequently accompanied them. Instead of regarding the quartering of soldiers as an unwelcome burden, towns were glad to receive a regiment because the soldiers' expenditures stimulated economic life. Berlin increased in population under Frederick William I from 60,000 to 100,000, of whom 20,000 were soldiers.

The army was a little world by itself, with its own laws, justice, and police. The soldier on furlough at home remained under the jurisdiction of his regiment and was not subject to the local court and police. Desertion was not uncommon; Frederick the Great advised generals not to take troops through a forest because it offered too good an opportunity for running away.

One of Frederick William's naïve hobbies was his regiment of "Potsdam giants." Composed of men well over six feet in height, and wearing a tall pointed headgear above their powdered heads, they formed one of the military sights of Europe. In addition to flint-lock and dagger, they carried a bag of hand grenades, and hence were known as grenadiers. As Prussia could not furnish enough "tall fellows," they were recruited anywhere in Europe they could be found—a practice that involved the king in several diplomatic conflicts with his neighbors. Some astute rulers gained his goodwill by presenting him with giants; Peter the Great sent him several, and Frederick William returned the compliment by humoring the Tsar's pet hobby by the gift of a small yacht.

As the Potsdam giants were expensive to recruit and maintain Frederick William established a special Recruit Chest (*Rekrutenkasse*). Its revenues at first consisted of payments for royal acts of grace such as pardons and permission to marry within forbidden relationships, and also of a quarter of the first year's pay of newly appointed officers. This financial device was similar to the Great Elector's *Chargenkasse* (see above, p. 72), with which the Recruit Chest was merged in 1722. Anyone seeking an appointment to any civil office was advised to make a donation to the Recruit Chest; if the donation was not generous, the candidate was not likely to get the coveted appointment. This practice, which smacks of bribery and the sale of public offices, did not have such evil consequences as one might expect, because of the king's ever-vigilant eye for laxity or corruption in office. Frederick the Great restricted the practice and abolished the Potsdam giants, believing that they were not worth what they cost and that men above normal size do not have more endurance or make better soldiers than men of average stature.

To improve efficiency, the wooden ramrod, which was liable to break or catch fire, was replaced by an iron one. The bayonet, which had hitherto been fastened into the muzzle of the gun and had to be removed before firing, was now fastened outside the barrel, so that soldiers could advance close to the enemy and continue firing and then instantly use the cold steel without delaying to fix bayonets. A state gun factory at Potsdam and a woolen mill at Berlin provided the army with a better single standard gun and proper uniforms. Frequent drills and maneuvers under Frederick William's exacting eye gave the troops quickness and precision of movement. These were extended by Frederick the Great into general autumn maneuvers and war games that gave the King the opportunity to judge the ability of his officers and to increase efficiency by weeding out the unfit and promoting the capable. He also developed the "oblique order" of attack, enabling a small army to defeat a much larger one by suddenly falling upon its flank.

By these improvements, as well as by his own genius for tactics and strategy, Frederick the Great was able to defeat half of Europe in the three Silesian Wars. At Hohenfriedberg in 1745, 58,000 Prussians routed 85,000 Saxons and Austrians, taking more than 7000 captives and 66 cannon. At Rossbach on November 5, 1757, 22,000 Prussians annihilated 43,000 Austrians, French, and imperialists; and just a month later, at Leuthen, 30,000 Prussians, by using the oblique order, rolled up 80,000 Austrians into a disastrous defeat.

Within fifteen years, in 1755, Frederick the Great doubled the army of 83,000 that he had inherited from his father. At the time of his death in 1786, he had increased it to 200,000 men, and it was generally regarded as the best disciplined and most efficient fighting force in Europe.

The Accession of Frederick the Great

Frederick the Great's life falls into three nearly equal periods: his youth and preparation for kingship until he was twenty-eight; the first half of his reign from 1740 to 1763 when he disturbed the peace of Europe by his three Silesian Wars; and the second twenty-three years of his rule when he sought to preserve the peace and *status quo* of Germany, lest he lose the Silesian prize that he had won. To be sure, in this third period he partitioned Poland and then waged the "Potato War" to prevent Joseph II of Austria from territorial aggrandizement, but essentially he aimed at peace, just as Bismarck a century later, having fought three wars to establish German unity, became after 1871 a man of peace to preserve what he had secured.

Frederick's youth had been most unhappy and embittered. Loving music and French poetry, he had been forbidden these by his brutal prosaic father. Frederick hated his father's coarse family tyranny, his religious zeal, his financial stinginess, and his naïve submission to the intrigues of the Austrian minister who completely pulled the wool over his eyes. Frederick felt his situation to be so intolerable that he finally tried to escape to England. He was caught in the act. His father, in boundless rage, considered putting him to death as a deserter from the sacred Prussian army, but eventually listened to the Emperor's plea for mercy, and merely imprisoned Fritz in the fortress of Küstrin.

After a year Frederick William I's wrath cooled. He decided to give Fritz a chance to redeem himself by giving him command of a regiment and local administrative work. In this new life the crown prince did his best to live up to his father's military and economical standards. He even accepted with dumb filial obedience a wife selected for him by his father, at the instigation of the Austrian minister, who thereby prevented a marriage alliance between Prussia and England. Frederick was never really in love with his wife, never had any children by her, and after he became king ceased to live with her; but otherwise he treated her with respect and consideration.

In 1736 Frederick William I relented further, and provided his son and daughter-in-law with a pleasant estate at Rheinsberg to the northwest of Berlin. Here Fritz continued to win his father's esteem by the skill and success with which he managed the estate. In return he was allowed to indulge himself to his heart's content in music, literature, and philosophy, and to have a select round table of cultured friends. The four years at Rheinsberg were the happiest of Frederick the Great's life. He read enormously, often sixteen or twenty hours a day. He stored his mind with classical French literature and with the writings of the Greeks and Romans in French translation. He took up philosophy, studied the campaigns of Caesar and Alexander the Great, and steeped his mind in the works of Machiavelli, Locke, Voltaire, Montesquieu, Leibniz, and the fashionable German philosopher Wolff. He wrote poetry, played the flute, and began a correspondence with Voltaire and other famous writers. His *L'Antimachiavel,* published anonymously in 1740, was a brilliant refutation of the Italian's principles of statecraft; it expressed Frederick's idealism and high moral philosophy—which he threw to the winds when dynastic interests and personal ambition impelled him to invade Silesia in the first year of his reign.

In these four happy Rheinsberg years Frederick made up for the deficiencies of his earlier education. He became one of the most cultured and best informed princes of Europe. Though he did not have the advantage of travel abroad, he had a far more accurate and enlightened knowledge of the lands and rulers of Europe than many more widely traveled persons. By hard study and the earnest application of a naturally brilliant mind, he matured himself to assume the duties of kingship. He learned to appreciate the sterling qualities by which his father, in spite of his crotchety tyranny, had built up for Prussia a large army and a substantial surplus treasure. And the father on his side regained complete confidence in his heir, declaring on the eve of his death on May 31,

1740, that he died content, "being sure of such a worthy son and successor."

Frederick II's first declaration of policy was an instruction to his civil servants that they were not to seek to enrich him by oppressing his subjects, but to have a single eye to the well-being of his country. He issued an edict abolishing torture, except in cases of treason and murder. He did away with the cruel practice by which mothers who killed their infants were sewn in sacks and drowned. He proclaimed absolute religious toleration, saying that all religions were equally good, provided their adherents were honest people, and that if Turks or heathen wanted to come and populate his lands he would build mosques and churches for them. He revived his grandfather's Academy of Sciences, appointed distinguished new members to it, and took an active personal part in its proceedings. By such initial measures the philosopher-king announced the era of enlightened despotism that was to characterize his reign and of which more will be said later.

Frederick the Great's Silesian Wars (1740–1763)

Five months after Frederick II became King, Emperor Charles VI of Austria died unexpectedly at Vienna on October 20, 1740, leaving a daughter, Maria Theresa, but no sons. As a woman had never ruled in the Hapsburg lands, Charles VI had spent his last years in seeking to make sure that her succession would be everywhere recognized. To effect this he had drawn up the Pragmatic Sanction, which had been sworn to by the Estates of each of his lands and had been accepted by all of the principal European rulers including the King of Prussia. No sooner had Charles VI died, however, than several princes, on one pretext or another, refused to recognize Maria Theresa's rights. The Elector of Bavaria laid claim to certain Hapsburg lands and even got himself elected Emperor in 1742. Frederick II, for his part, instantly decided to seize possession of the rich Hapsburg province of Silesia.

Frederick's motives were several. He felt that Prussia had long been duped by Austria. His father had been led around by the nose by the Austrian minister at Berlin who had reported to Vienna that Frederick William I was a poltroon who would never dare to fight. Frederick II wanted to show that Prussia could assert herself as one of the great powers of Europe. He also burned to imitate the heroic deeds of which he had read so much and thus win personal glory. Therefore when he went to put himself at the head of his troops in Silesia, he left at home his most experienced general, old Leopold of Dessau, saying: "I don't want the world to say that when the King of Prussia goes to war he takes a tutor at his elbow." Moreover, the European situation seemed favorable: England was at war with Spain since 1739, and he believed that, in view of the long-standing enmity between the Bourbons and the Hapsburgs, he could secure France as an ally.

Frederick also saw the opportunity to make good claims that the Hohenzollerns had long had to half a dozen little counties in Silesia, but which the Hapsburgs had refused to recognize. Rather than negotiate for these in Vienna, he believed it shrewder to seize the whole of Silesia and negotiate afterwards. Silesia would form a very valuable acquisition of territory. Lying in the valley of the Oder, it had more than a million inhabitants, with thriving linen and other industries using the water power from the little streams that flow from the Bohemian or Sudeten Mountains into the Oder. Though jutting out like an appendage to Brandenburg to the southeast, Silesia was really more closely connected with Brandenburg by the valley of the Oder than with Bohemia across the mountains to the west or with the Polish plains to the east. Two canals linked the Oder to the Spree, Havel, and Elbe, with Berlin at the center of the water transportation system. As to Prussia's promise to respect the Pragmatic Sanction, that might be disregarded because Austria had not kept her promise to support Prussia's claims to Jülich and Berg, whose ruler had recently died without direct heirs. The legal claims to the half dozen little counties in Silesia were to Frederick of secondary importance; they were chiefly valuable as affording a plausible pretext to the world for his action. As he wrote to his Minister of Foreign Affairs, Podewils: "The legal question is an affair for you ministers, and it is time to work it up secretly, for the orders to the troops have been issued."

By the middle of December 1740 the Prussian columns were on the march toward Silesia. On the twelfth Frederick II gave a masquerade ball at the Berlin Schloss, and went from it to place himself at the head of his troops without giving the least hint of the stroke he had been preparing in secret for seven weeks. On the 16th, thinking of Caesar as he entered Silesia, he wrote joyously to Podewils: "We have crossed the Rubicon, with flags flying and music playing." The first weeks of the campaign were an easy military promenade for the young king and his troops, because Maria Theresa had been taken wholly by surprise and had only a few scattered garrison troops in Silesia. The strong fortress of Glogau was taken by assault on March 8. Breslau, the capital of Silesia, opened its gates in view of Frederick's promises of religious toleration and the strict discipline maintained by his troops. His armies were then able to occupy the whole province.

By April 1741, however, Maria Theresa had had time to recover from her surprise. Austrian troops filtered across the mountain passes from Bohemia into Silesia and threatened to cut off the widely scattered Prussian forces from their line of communications with Brandenburg. Frederick ordered his scattered troops to retreat quickly toward Breslau. On April 9 they found their way blocked near Mollwitz by an equal number of Austrians and rushed to attack. But the Prussian troops began to fire too soon, became disorganized, and appeared to be defeated. Frederick, rushing forward, was in such imminent danger of being captured that his general, Schwerin, persuaded him to flee to the rear. He spent a bitter, desolate night, riding about trying to collect more troops. After he had left the field, however, Schwerin managed to rally the Prussians and turned Mollwitz from a defeat into a victory. It was a mortifying episode for the King who had set out to win military glory and emulate Caesar and Alexander the Great. But it taught him valuable lessons: that the field of battle is very different from the parade ground; that actual fighting is necessary to make good soldiers; and that a commander ought not to risk his life at the forefront of his troops but stay toward the rear to direct their movements.

The Prussian victory at Mollwitz was a surprise to Europe. It had been generally expected that the Austrians would effectively punish Frederick for what was regarded as a treacherous and foolhardy invasion. On the day the battle was fought, Austria, Saxony, and Hanover had formed a coalition against him, and if he had been defeated would probably have partitioned some of his lands. Such was the political morality of the eighteenth century. From an ethical point of view Frederick was little better or worse than his neighbors. He differed from them in that he was able to succeed where they failed. The most important political result of Mollwitz was that the French now decided to enter into alliance with him, and soon sent an army to aid the Bavarians in their attack upon Maria Theresa.

Strengthened by the French and Bavarians, Frederick was able to persuade the hard-pressed Austrians to sign the Convention of Klein-Schnellendorf on October 9, 1741: Maria Theresa ceded to him most of Silesia, and the

Austrian troops, after a sham engagement, were to with-
draw from Silesia. The convention was to be kept secret to
veil the fact that Frederick was leaving his allies in the
lurch. The Austrian troops were then free to occupy
Bavaria and deprive the Elector of his own capital at
Munich two weeks after he had been elected Emperor
Charles VII. Frederick, fearing that he might be attacked
next, suddenly decided to reopen hostilities, alleging as a
pretext that the Austrians had not kept the Convention of
Klein-Schnellendorf secret as stipulated. He invaded Bohemia and, by a brilliant flank attack on the Austrian left
wing, won the Battle of Chotusitz on May 17, 1742.
Leaving his allies again in the lurch, he then compelled
Maria Theresa, by the Peace of Breslau on July 28, to cede
the whole of Silesia. This ended successfully for him the
First Silesian War, but the general European War of the
Austrian Succession, started by his action, was continued
by the other participants until 1748.

Freed for the moment from the Prussian menace, Maria
Theresa expelled the French and Bavarians from Bohemia, routed a second French army at Dettingen near
Frankfort-on-the-Main in 1743, and was ready to attempt
the reconquest of Silesia. Fearing this, Frederick began a
"preventive war" to crush her before she became strong
enough to regain her lost province. In this Second Silesian
War of 1744–1745 he invaded Bohemia through Saxony,
but failed to capture Prague and had to retreat into Silesia
for winter quarters. In 1745 he purposely allowed the
Austrians and Saxons to file through the mountain passes
from Bohemia into Silesia. "If you want to catch a mouse,
don't shut the mousetrap," he said significantly to a
French friend. Deceiving the enemy forces by a feigned
hasty retreat, he suddenly advanced by a night march to a
surprise attack at dawn. By eight o'clock on the morning
of June 4 at Hohenfriedberg, 58,000 Prussians had completely routed 85,000 Austrians and Saxons, capturing

7000 prisoners and killing or wounding nearly 7000 more. Frederick's own loss was only 900 killed and some 4000 wounded. "The old Romans have done nothing more brilliant," he wrote to the faithful Podewils. In jubilation Frederick composed the "Hohenfriedberg March" and dedicated it to the Prussian army—a thoroughly creditable piece of martial music which has remained very popular in Germany ever since. After further victories Frederick entered Dresden, the Saxon capital, and there, on Christmas day, dictated peace. Again Maria Theresa had to acknowledge him as the ruler of Silesia, and Saxony had to pay a million talers war indemnity.

During the next ten years he increased the army to more than 150,000 and gathered funds for a possible new war. Maria Theresa likewise reformed and enlarged her army, learning by the example of Prussia. She reorganized her government and finances in the direction of greater centralization, somewhat as the Hohenzollerns had been doing for a century. She made new secret alliances with Russia and Saxony, and by the "diplomatic revolution" was planning to ally herself with the ancient Hapsburg enemy, France, in place of the ineffective friendship with England. Frederick, scenting danger and knowing that France and England would always be on opposite sides, hastened to ally himself with England and abandon the fifteen-year old French alliance.

In August 1756 Frederick II opened the Third Silesian War by an unsuccessful attempt to invade Bohemia through the Saxon Mountains. The life-and-death struggle between Prussia and Austria that followed was only one part of the wider so-called Seven Years' War that was fought all over Europe, on the high seas, and in the colonies. Frederick had to face the larger part of Europe almost single-handed, because the English did not keep all their subsidy promises and gave him no effective support. Though he won brilliant victories over French and German forces at Rossbach on November 5, 1757, and again over the Austrians at Leuthen in Silesia just a month later, the numerical odds were terribly against him, and the strain upon his nerves and resources was frightful. In the following years it was worse, because the Russians marched through East Prussia to the Oder and slaughtered thousands of Prussian soldiers in bloody encounter at Zorndorf in 1758 and at Kunersdorf in 1759. These were the black days when Frederick carried a vial of poison hidden on his person so that the King of Prussia should not be captured alive.

In 1762, however, the Russian danger was removed by the death of the hostile Empress Elizabeth and the accession of the friendly Peter III. Austria meanwhile was almost as exhausted as Prussia. As Maria Theresa's chief ally France had been everywhere defeated by England, she at last abandoned hopes of reconquering Silesia. By the Treaty of Hubertusburg on February 15, 1763, she renounced the rich province in favor of the Hohenzollerns for all time.

By the Silesian Wars Frederick had proved himself a military genius and an excellent administrator. To appreciate his tactics and strategy one should read the accounts in Thomas Carlyle's enthusiastic *History of Frederick the Great,* in the official Prussian General Staff History, or in Frederick's own *Histoire de mon Temps, Guerre de Sept Ans,* and *Oeuvres Militaires.* By his administrative skill he managed to finance the wars without incurring foreign debts as did his neighbors. He did, to be sure, depreciate the coinage and pay his bills in paper promises, but as soon as the war was over he restored the coinage almost to its prewar value and redeemed the paper. He even came out of the war with a considerable reserve in the war-chest, from which he made a great many gifts or loans at low interest to help "reestablish" his war-impoverished subjects. Silesia, with its

1,180,000 relatively prosperous inhabitants, increased by nearly one-half the population of Prussia which in 1740 was still only about two and a half millions. After 1763 the rich deposits of coal, iron, lead, cobalt, and other minerals in Upper Silesia began to be gradually exploited and to furnish an increasingly large revenue. Silesia was allowed to keep most of its local institutions. Instead of being placed under the General Directory and integrated with the rest of the Prussian administrative system, it was placed under a special governor resident at Breslau and directly responsible to the King.

By the Silesian Wars Frederick helped to overcome the inferiority complex from which Germans generally had suffered since the helpless, humiliating days of the Thirty Years' War. By his brilliant victories, especially at Rossbach over the French, he had contributed to the awakening of German nationalism that was also beginning to find expression in the new German literature of Herder, Lessing, Wieland, and Klopstock. He had raised Prussia to the level of the Great Powers of Europe. People began to feel, as Mirabeau wrote in 1786: "Prussia is today, on the continent, the pivot of peace and war."

The Acquisition of West Prussia
(1772)

Frederick II returned to Berlin in 1763 tired in body and spirit, saddened by the strain imposed on his subjects by the war, and genuinely desirous of peace for the rest of his days. It was as if a bleak, sunless winter's day had followed the springlike warm enthusiasm and joyous self-confidence with which he had crossed the Rubicon in 1740. He now realized poignantly how close he had come to complete disaster during the critical period of the Seven Years' War. Prussia had been compelled to fight single-handed on three fronts against Austria, France, Russia, and several German princes. Frederick had won a defensive victory, but he knew by how narrow a margin. So, after being the chief disturber of the peace from 1740 to 1763, he now became its chief defender for the next twenty-three years. For he realized that Prussia, occupying a dangerous middle position between the three continental great powers, and having a long, exposed, and straggling frontier, was very vulnerable. In another general war he might not escape disaster a second time. After 1763, therefore, it was not he, but Catherine II of Russia and Joseph II of Austria who with their restless ambitions threatened the peace and *status quo* of Europe. Frederick's aim was to hold them in check by skillful diplomacy.

How could Frederick break the ring of enemies encircling him? Austria, smarting under the loss of Silesia, was likely to remain a potential danger. She was still guided by the astute Kaunitz who had arranged the alliance with France and was soon to cement it further by the marriage of Maria Theresa's daughter to the French dauphin. The French, moreover, had not forgotten that Frederick had thrice left them in the lurch. There remained Russia. The accession of Peter III in 1761 had been a heaven-sent piece of good luck for Frederick, but the next year Peter's wife profited by his assassination to mount the blood-stained throne as Catherine II. Coming from the little German principality of Anhalt-Zerbst that was overshadowed by Prussia, she at first disliked Frederick and began her reign by denouncing him as Russia's "mortal enemy." As heir to the policy of Peter the Great, she had great ambitions to extend her empire at the expense of Poland and Turkey, and thus threatened Frederick's policy of preserving peace and the *status quo.* Could he win her friendship without binding himself in an alliance with her which would involve him in an eastern war? He not only did so, but acquired another great province—at Poland's expense.

Frederick the Great, painting by Antoine Pesne.
(Kgl. Gallery, Berlin; Giraudon)

Catherine II of Russia, painting by Eric Ericksen. *(Giraudon)*

For a century Poland had been growing progressively weaker and was approaching a condition of chaos and anarchy. While the Hohenzollerns and Romanovs had checked the disintegrating tendency of the selfish nobility and had been building up a strong centralized government and princely absolutism in Prussia and Russia, a reverse process had been taking place in Poland. The Polish nobility had arrogated so many "liberties" to themselves that the king's power had shrunk to a shadow. The elective monarchy not only prevented any one dynasty from establishing its authority firmly, but invited bribery and interference by foreign powers at every election. The *liberum veto,* by which any one Polish deputy could block legislation and "rupture" the legislature, and the "right of confederation," by which any group of nobles could band together for common political and military action against the rest, promoted and virtually legalized civil war. Fanatical Roman Catholic oppression of the "dissidents" offered Catherine and Frederick a pretext to intervene on behalf of their respective Greek Orthodox and Protestant coreligionists.

The death of Augustus III, King of Poland and Elector of Saxony, on October 5, 1763, opened a new Polish crisis. Catherine II desired the election of her former lover, Stanislas Poniatowski, believing that she could still keep him in her leading strings and through him as king could practically rule all Poland. By supporting her candidate, Frederick II saw an opportunity to win her goodwill and to protect his own lands. In an alliance of April 11, 1764, therefore, Frederick and Catherine agreed to guarantee each other's territories, to aid each other if necessary with troops, and to back the election of Poniatowski. This was harmless enough. But they went on to the cynical mutual promise that they would prevent any reforms in Poland that might strengthen the disintegrating state, such as the establishment of a hereditary in place of an elective monarchy and the abolition of the *liberum veto*.

Six months later, under Russian pressure, Poniatowski was duly chosen king in what was regarded as a remarkably peaceful election: "only ten men were killed." The new king, however, soon cast off Catherine's leading strings and sought to adopt a national policy for strengthening Poland. Catherine, seeing that her calculation of dominating Poland through her ex-lover had miscarried, began to make trouble for him. She instigated malcontent Polish nobles to form a "confederation" against him, stirred up a peasant revolt in South Poland, and demanded concessions for the Greek Orthodox dissidents. In 1768 she sent Russian troops to support the "confederation" opposing Poniatowski. These troops marched over a corner of Turkish territory, which threw the Grand Vizier into a paroxysm of rage and caused a six-year Russo-Turkish War in which Catherine was overwhelmingly triumphant on land and sea.

Frederick the Great disapproved of all these high-handed acts of Catherine II, but remained complaisant for fear of antagonizing his only friend. To be sure, as a hint to her that there were limits to his complaisance, he had a couple of friendly interviews with his admirer Joseph II of Austria, who at this time was jealous of Russian expansion toward Constantinople.

As Austria and Prussia did not want Catherine to retain all the lands she had occupied in the war with Turkey, what happier solution than to compensate her with a large slice of Polish territory, now that Poniatowski would no longer do her bidding? Austria had seized the Polish district of Zips in 1770. Polish Prussia, as Frederick had privately pointed out when he was only nineteen—in a letter to his friend, Natzmer, in 1731—would be a most valuable acquisition for the Hohenzollerns. Why not have all three of Poland's powerful neighbors take coveted slices of her defenseless territory as an easy solution of the eastern question? The subject was mooted between Catherine and Frederick's brother Prince Henry on his visit to St. Petersburg, and quickly resulted in the First Partition of Poland in 1772.

Catherine took White Russia and Lithuania; Maria Theresa, protesting with tears against the iniquitous proceeding, nevertheless took Galicia; and Frederick joyfully received the wedge-shaped Bishopric of Ermeland in East Prussia and Polish, or West, Prussia but without Danzig and Thorn. Though his share was only one-third in size that of Catherine and one-half that of Maria Theresa, it was politically more important.

The partition gave Frederick II control of the valley of the Vistula highway. It united the eastern and central Hohenzollern lands in a solid continuous territory by connecting East Prussia with Pomerania and Brandenburg. It not only freed Prussia from the danger of further Russian attacks through Poland, but, since Prussia had now became *particeps criminis* with Russia in dismembering Poland, the Hohenzollerns and Romanovs were henceforth drawn together politically for more than a century by their common interest in preventing any restoration of Poland. It also increased Prussia's population by some 600,000 inhabitants, partly Germans, partly Poles, and partly doubtful Cassubians. Prussia recovered a territory that had been conquered and settled by the Teutonic Knights, but which had been taken from the Germans at their time of weakness and defeat in 1466.

The "Potato War" of 1778-1779, and the League of Princes

Joseph II became Emperor of the Holy Roman Empire and joint-ruler with his mother, Maria Theresa, in 1765. An enlightened despot like Frederick II and Catherine II, he was eager to reform and strengthen his miscellaneous lands and play a leading role. In 1778, upon the death of the Elector of Bavaria without direct heirs, he made a secret treaty with the next Wittelsbach claimant, Charles Theodore of the Palatinate, who had no legitimate children but plenty of illegitimate ones of whom he was personally fond. Joseph agreed to provide pensions for the bastards, and in return was to get a third of Bavaria, which he at once occupied with troops. But another Wittelsbach heir, Charles of Zweibrücken, protested the arrangement that would deprive him of some of his ultimate inheritance. Alone, he was helpless.

Frederick the Great, however, immediately championed the rights of Zweibrücken and stood forth as the defender of the Germanic constitution and the *status quo*. Under cover of generous disinterestedness, he wished to prevent such an increase of Austrian territory and power as would upset the balance in Germany and possibly encourage Joseph II to attempt to recover Silesia. When Joseph paid no heed to his demands for the withdrawal of Austrian troops from Bavaria, Frederick sent a Prussian army under his brother into Bohemia. Owing to lack of energy and to mistakes, Prince Henry avoided battle. Both armies merely maneuvered until winter came on, when the Prussians withdrew again into Silesia. The soldiers, who had been occupied chiefly in finding provisions, derisively dubbed this War of the Bavarian Succession the "Potato War." In the following year, Russian and France, allies respectively of Prussia and Austria, mediated a compromise settlement by the Peace of Teschen of May 13, 1779. Austria kept the Innviertel, a small corner of Bavaria east of the Inn, but withdrew her troops and abandoned all claims to the rest of the Bavarian inheritance. Frederick had essentially succeeded in his main purpose of thwarting any great increase of Hapsburg power.

In 1780, with the death of Maria Theresa, Joseph II became sole ruler of Austria and was more free to indulge in his program of "enlightened" reforms. By visiting and flattering Catherine II, and by planning with her a joint spoliation of Turkey, he secured her favor just as Frederick began to lose it by his pro-Turkish attitude. Encouraged by this shift in the European diplomatic situation, Joseph II suddenly announced in 1784 his bold project of giving the complaisant Charles Theodore the faraway, restless Austrian Netherlands and receiving from him in exchange the contiguous Bavarian Electorate. Again Charles of Zweibrücken protested, and again Frederick the Great championed his rights, this time not by force as in 1778, but by the formation of a League of Princes (*Fürstenbund*).

The *Fürstenbund,* composed at first of the three principal north German states—Prussia, Saxony, and Hanover—was soon joined by fourteen others, great and small, Protestant and Catholic. Its purpose was to protect the Germanic constitution and the *status quo.* Supported diplomatically by France, which by the Peace of Westphalia was also one of the guarantors of the Germanic constitution, it effectively blocked Joseph II's high-handed Bavarian Exchange Plan. It has sometimes been represented as a first step in the Prussian unification of Germany that was to be achieved later by Bismarck. In reality, the *Fürstenbund* did not aim at the creation of a new nation but the conservation of an outworn medieval mosaic, by winning to the side of Prussia other German princes who were frightened by Joseph II's revolutionary ambitions. It was Frederick's final diplomatic success. On August 17, 1786, the lonely old man, idolized by posterity as "der alte Fritz," closed his eyes at Postdam, little dreaming how the revolutionary flood from France was soon to expose the weaknesses of the state he had governed for forty-six years.

Frederick the Great
as Enlightened Despot

Frederick II, whom other monarchs and their ministers of the latter eighteenth century sought to emulate, was the most distinguished representative of what is called enlightened despotism. This was based on the idea that the king, having studied the enlightened doctrines of the *philosophes,* knew better than his subjects what was for their good, and that he had, or should have, the despotic power to carry out reforms, not for his own glory, but for the well-being of his people and the advantage of his state.

"I am the first servant of the state," was Frederick's oft-repeated motto. When a delegation of townspeople came to thank him for a generous donation of money which he had made to enable them to rebuild their houses destroyed by fire, Frederick, "visibly moved," replied characteristically: "You have no need to thank me; it was my duty; that is what I am here for." The justification of his absolute authority, he believed, did not rest upon the grace of God, divine right, or dynastic inheritance, but upon the natural law theory of the social contract—upon his ability to serve his people better than they could serve themselves.

The Enlightened Despotism of the latter eighteenth century was very different from the absolutism of the Age of Louis XIV. The "great monarch" of France exalted his own personal glory, considering himself the source of all radiance and light, and choosing as his symbol the rising sun. He constituted the whole state according to the maxim which Voltaire put into his mouth: *L'état, c'est moi.* His will was law: *Si veut le Roi, si veut la Loi.* In the well-being of his subjects, whom he exhausted by long wars and oppressed with heavy taxation, he took relatively little interest. His government was neither *by* the people nor *for* the people.

Frederick the Great, on the other hand, as enlightened despot, marked a great step forward. He distinguished between himself as the servant of the state and the Prussian state itself. "The Ruler is the first servant of the state; he is well paid so that he may uphold the dignity of his position." Like Montesquieu, he believed that the monarch was subject to the law. In his *Political Testament* of 1752 he wrote: "I have resolved never to interfere with the course of legal procedure; for in the halls of justice the laws shall speak and the monarch shall keep silence." In the famous Miller Arnold case, where he broke this resolution, he did so because he believed—incorrectly—that a noble, backed by unjust judges, had done a great wrong to a poor peasant. If he exacted oppressive taxes, he did not spend them on costly robes to replace his simple blue uniform, soiled with dust and snuff, but returned a large part of them, even amounting to a quarter of his revenues in the years following the Seven Years' War, in free gifts for the amelioration and well-being of his subjects. His reforms, imposed with moderation from above, served in some sort as a lightning rod that drew off discontent and averted in Prussia violent reform by the masses from below, such as took place in France soon after his death. His was a government *for* the people, if not *by* the people. Indeed, he frequently expressed his utter contempt for human nature, and obviously believed that mankind was incapable of governing itself.

Frederick was a man of action rather than an organizer. He did not greatly change the framework of centralized institutions that he inherited from his father. He did, however, in actual practice gather much more power directly into his own hands, and left less freedom of action to his ministers. The members of the General Directory rarely reported to him in person, or even saw him, except once a year when the budget was drawn up. The reports of the various boards sitting in Berlin were sent to him at

Sans Souci in Potsdam in writing, and he gave his decisions by dictating to his cabinet secretaries or by jotting down marginal notes from which they prepared his "cabinet orders." The amount and variety of the business which he thus dealt with is almost incredible. A fraction of it which has been published fills forty-four volumes of his *Politische Korrespondenz* and a score of volumes of the *Acta Borussica*. His working day began at 6 A.M. In the evenings he sought recreation in music, playing the flute to the round table of select friends, or in reading, in discussing philosophy, or in catching up on his literary writings and correspondence that comprise the thirty-three volumes of his *Oeuvres*.

In addition to this daily routine at Sans Souci and to commanding his troops in the Silesian Wars, Frederick made frequent journeys of inspection through his provinces. He talked with nobles, burghers, peasants, and local officials, noting down with neat precision all sorts of statistics in the little red leather notebooks which he always carried with him. This information gathered on the spot enabled him to check up on the reports of his ministers, spend money where he was convinced it was needed, and inspire everywhere his own sense of duty and hard work. If his sharp eye detected corruption, incompetence or insubordination, instant dismissal and a year's imprisonment at Spandau were likely to be the offender's fate.

Frederick II's minute personal direction of every branch of the government had its advantages. Decisions by the King were far more speedy than by majority votes after long discussions by boards of ministers. Secrecy, where desirable, could more easily be maintained. All responsibility was centered in himself. As in his campaigns he never called a council of war, so in administration in general he saw no need for similar assemblies for discussion and advice. By this example, by his extraordinarily wide knowledge and mastery of detail, and by the fear of disapprobation which he inspired he carried further his father's work of educating Prussian military officials and civil servants to severe standards of duty, honesty, efficiency, and impartial justice which for a century and a half were to make the army and the bureaucracy the two solid pillars of the Prussian state. His system, however, had also its disadvantages. It could be completely successful in the long run only if his successors equaled him in genius— which was not the case. Like Bismarck, he expected obedience, not initiative and independent responsibility, in his officials. He did not develop ministers of outstanding ability who could take over his autocratic machinery of government when his guiding hand was removed.

With the disappearance at the Reformation of the clergy as one of the "three estates" of the Middle Ages, the nobles, burghers, and peasants came to form the threefold division of society in Brandenburg-Prussia. This division was retained by Frederick II, and even sharpened by his social measures and by the provisions of his Prussian Law Code.

The nobility, instead of offering a narrow-minded local opposition to the Hohenzollern centralized monarchy, had now become its main and loyal support. No longer fearing the selfish political ambitions of the Junkers, Frederick extended their powers and privileges. In his name they exercised wide police powers on their landed estates. They were appointed more exclusively to officer positions in the army, for Frederick believed that they had a higher sense of honor than the middle and lower classes, and in any case they were used to commanding the peasants on their estates who formed the bulk of the recruits for the army.

The burghers were expected to serve the state, not by fighting, but by increasing its wealth through industry and trade. Consequently, after the Seven Years' War, they were not appointed officers and were exempted from being recruited as soldiers under the cantonal system. To promote internal trade and industry, Frederick II followed the usual mercantilist methods of excluding foreign manufactures by tariffs and by restricting the exportation of raw materials. He also swept away many internal tolls, especially those on the Oder which with the acquisition of Silesia had now become a water highway wholly within the Prussian boundaries. He established new monopolies for tobacco, porcelain, silk, and other manufactures. He stimulated other industries by generous subventions from his *Dispositionskasse*. With the assistance of his able Minister of Mines, Heinitz, he began to develop the mineral resources of Upper Silesia. Shipbuilding began to flourish at Stettin; in a single year twenty ships were launched, some of which were sold abroad. In 1765, with the advice of an Italian, Calzabigi, he founded a Prussian Bank with a capital of 400,000 talers to aid recovery after the Seven Years' War. It received deposits, made loans, discounted paper bills, and later issued paper money. By 1786 it was making an annual profit of 22,000 talers.

According to statistics furnished by Heinitz in 1783, Prussia's annual exports amounted to 14,800,000 talers and her imports to 11,800,000, making a favorable balance of 3,000,000. Her manufactures had a total annual value of 29,000,000 talers, as follows:

Manufactures (not including Silesia)	Workers	Home Consumption	Exported
		(value in talers)	
Silk	5,055	1,356,702	531,026
Woolens	39,367	3,344,166	1,691,305
Linen	22,523	373,506	897,757
Leather	3,595	996,614	399,986
Cotton	4,503	540,056	106,765
Iron and glass	8,373	2,126,675	1,053,844
Totals	83,416	8,737,719	4,606,683

Total home consumption and exports, approximately	13,500,000
Paper, tobacco, sugar, porcelain, tallow, soap	4,500,000
Silesian woolens, linen, iron, steel, lead, etc.	11,000,000
Total Prussian manufactures	29,000,000

In spite of this considerable industrialization under Frederick the Great, which raised Prussia to be the fourth manufacturing country of the world, Prussia still remained essentially an agrarian state, and the peasantry still bore the chief burden of the political and social order. Their sons were recruited for the rank and file of the army, which had increased to 200,000 in 1786. The heavy military land tax was assessed exclusively on peasant land holdings, except in East Prussia and Silesia where the land of the nobles also bore a part. In addition, the peasants had to perform labor services of three of four days a week for their overlords, not to mention services to the State such as building roads, transporting troops, and doing errands for officials and army officers. The peasant was, as Frederick the Great said, "the beast of burden of human society."

Frederick II attempted to do something to ameliorate the peasants' hard lot but refused to attack serfdom as such. On his own domain lands, which constituted about a third of the kingdom, he succeeded in assuring them heredity of tenure, in limiting in writing the nature and amount of their labor services, and in some cases in abolishing the obligation of menial service on the part of the peasants' sons and daughters. On the private estates of the nobles, however, he found that traditional custom and bitter opposition on the part of the Junker landlords were too strong for him to accomplish much. The only important reform he was able to achieve here was the prevention of *Bauernlegung,* which was the prying of the peasant off of his tenement so that the lord might add the peasant's acre strips to his own demesne lands.

To improve agriculture Frederick sent agents to England to study the better methods coming into use there. As a result he taught his own subjects to make greater use of fodder crops and of clover which enriched the soil instead of impoverishing it. It also made possible more feeding of cattle in the stalls instead of in the fields, improved the quality and amount of milk, and produced more stable manure that could be used further to enrich the fields. He persuaded his people to make greater use of such cheap forms of food as potatoes and turnips. He adopted better methods of cattle breeding, so that the number of sheep was increased from 5,500,000 in 1765 to 8,000,000 in 1786, making possible a considerable export of wool.

Frederick II began the systematic planting and care of pines and firs that gave Germany a leading place in modern forestry methods. To increase available agricultural land, he carried out extensive drainage projects, especially in the regions of the lower Oder and Vistula. These two rivers were connected by the Bromberg canal, thus making a direct east-west cheap water transportation between East Prussia and the central provinces. Like the Great Elector who settled 20,000 French Huguenots and like Frederick William I who provided traveling expenses, land, and livestock for an equal number of exiled Salzburg Protestants, Frederick the Great was very active in colonization work. Not having at hand any such convenient bands of religious exiles, he sought his colonists in little groups from all over Germany and from neighboring foreign lands. In the course of his whole reign he far exceeded the work of his predecessors by settling a total of 300,000 colonists.

Frederick's grain policy was much the same as that of the Great Elector, but was pursued on a much larger scale. Generally the exportation and importation of grain was forbidden, though he sometimes allowed his own grain officials to import under cover from Poland. With the frontiers generally closed to grain, Frederick bought up and stored in government warehouses wheat, barley, and rye in plentiful years when the price was low, and sold it again in years of bad harvest when prices tended to rise and would otherwise have caused great hardship to consumers. In this way he succeeded in his aim of keeping a fairly stable price level for grain and at the same time made a handsome profit.

In the intervals between his wars, and partly to aid recovery by public works, Frederick built many prominent public buildings in Berlin. The Opera House in 1743 was one of the first. Near it, on the same side of the Unter den Linden promenade, he constructed a library to house the growing collection of books which the Great Elector had started, and, a little to the rear, the Church of St. Hedwig for his Roman Catholic subjects. Across the Linden from the Opera House he erected a large palace for his brother, Prince Henry, which is now occupied by the Humboldt University of East Berlin.

One of Frederick's most important achievements was the reform and codification of the law. His father had made efforts at legal reform, but he had been too impatient, too ignorant of the fundamental difficulties, and too strongly opposed by the Junker justices to accomplish much. Frederick's success was largely due to Samuel von Cocceji. This able lawyer and skillful organizer had been dismissed by Frederick William I, but was restored to office by Frederick the Great. He raised the quality of the judges by giving them better pay, instead of having them largely dependent on gifts from the litigants. He simplified the long and costly Roman written procedure by restricting appeals and by making greater use of the Germanic oral procedure. He made use of the period of his enforced idleness, after his dismissal by Frederick William I, in drafting a code of simplified law to harmonize the practice in the different provinces. In 1751 he translated his Latin draft into German. During the next forty years other eminent lawyers and judges worked on it, and it was the basis of the Prussian Code finally put into practice in 1794.

Frederick the Great's reign is the culmination of a century and a half of extraordinary development of the Brandenburg-Prussian state. From a weak Electorate it had risen to be the strongest military state in Germany, with a population little smaller than that of England. A glance at four of the factors which the eighteenth century regarded as decisive for state strength will show the striking progress in this century and a half from the end of the Thirty Years' War to the death of Frederick the Great:

	1648	1740	1786
Population	750,000	2,500,000	5,000,000
Army	8,000	83,000	200,000
Annual revenues, in talers	?	7,000,000	19,000,000
Stored treasure, in talers	0	8,000,000	51,000,000

Under Frederick the Great Prussia had become the powerful rival of Austria, and, by accentuating the dualism in the Holy Roman Empire had, in spite of Frederick's efforts at conservation at the time of the *Fürstenbund* in 1785, actually hastened the disruption of that decaying medieval structure.

The Great Elector and Frederick William I had been fertile in creating new institutions and in organizing the resources of their lands. Frederick the Great added valuable new lands, but created little that was new in the way of institutions, being content to use and develop those that he inherited. However, by his demonic energy, his shrewd estimate of Prussia's interests, and his successful opportunism, he did more than either of his predecessors to raise Prussia high in importance as a European state. But Prussia still remained a despotic state, such as was characteristic of the eighteenth century. Unfortunately Frederick's genius as an enlightened despot was not a heritable quality to be transmitted to his immediate successors. It required the shock of the Napoleonic conquest and the genius of Freiherr vom Stein to bring about a new creative period of institutional changes that were to regenerate and further strengthen Prussia in the nineteenth century.

Bibliographical Note

The main bibliographical guide is F. C. Dahlmann and **G.** Waitz, *Quellenkunde der Deutschen Geschichte* (9th ed., Leipzig, 1932) [a new edition now in preparation]. For the Medieval period L. J. Paetow, *A Guide to the Study of Medieval History* (New York, 1931) is still indispensable. Current literature is reviewed with commendable promptness in the *American Historical Review* and *Journal of Modern History*, with inexcusable tardiness in the *Historische Zeitschrift*. Most of the recent literature is cited in Bruno Gebhardt, *Handbuch der deutschen Geschichte*. Volume II: *Von der Reformation bis zum Ende des Absolutismus* (8th ed., Stuttgart, 1955). The pertinent sections are written by Professor Max Braubach of Bonn University, one of the world's greatest living authorities on the period.

Of the general histories of Prussia the best is A. Waddington *Histoire de Prusse* (2 vols., Paris, 1911–1922), scholarly, very readable and well arranged, but comes only to 1740. The best German shorter account is O. Hintze, *Die Hohenzollern und ihr Werk* (Berlin, 1915), especially valuable for social and institutional history. A propagandist pamphlet of gigantic dimensions and prodigious research from which all subsequent writers draw much material is J. G. Droysen, *Geschichte der Preussischen Politik* (5 parts in 14 vols., Leipzig, 1855–1886); it aimed, by showing the superiority of Prussia over Austria, to promote the unification of Germany under Prussian leadership as accomplished by Bismarck, but breaks off at 1757 with the author's death in 1884. A good corrective to Droysen is H. Prutz, *Preussische Geschichte* (4 vols., Stuttgart, 1900–1902). H. Tuttle, *History of Prussia* (4 vols., Boston, 1884–1896) gives attention to institutions, is somewhat dull and unsympathetic, and like Droysen stops in the middle of the Seven Years' War owing to the author's death. Leopold von Ranke, *History of Prussia* (3 vols., London, 1847–1848), conservative and Lutheran in point of view, is still useful as political history. The first volume of Thomas Carlyle's *History of Frederick the Great* (6 vols., London, 1858–1865) gives a piquant and often amusing survey of his hero's predecessors for six centuries. The best brief history of Prussia in English is C. Robertson and J. Marriott, *The Evolution of Prussia* (Oxford, 1917).

For the constitutional and legal history of Germany as a whole the two best manuals are F. Hartung, *Deutsche Verfassungsgeschichte* (7th ed., Stuttgart, 1959), and R. Schröder, *Lehrbuch der deutschen Rechtsgeschichte* (6th ed., Leipzig, 1922). The Brandenburg-Prussian electoral and royal edicts, systematically classified, were edited by C. O. Mylius, *Corpus Constitutionum Marchicarum* (8 vols. in folio, Berlin and Halle, 1736–1741). The political views and testamentary instructions of Hohenzollern rulers are printed with comments by H. von Caemmerer, *Die Testamente der Kurfürsten von Brandenburg und der beiden ersten Könige von Preussen* (Munich and Berlin, 1915).

The survey of financial institutions by A. F. Riedel, *Der Brandenburgisch-Preussische Staatshaushalt* (Berlin, 1866) is valuable for its full statistical tables of receipts and expenditures from 1608 to 1806.

The organization and the development of the army, with some account of military history, is definitely treated by C. Jany, *Geschichte der Königlich Preussischen Armee* (4 vols., Berlin, 1928–1933).

CHAPTER 1

In addition to the general histories of Prussia mentioned above, one of the best surveys to 1648 is R. Koser, *Geschichte der brandenburgischen Politik* (Stuttgart and Berlin, 1913).

G. Schmoller, *The Mercantile System and its Historical Significance* (New York, 1896) shows how economic and political factors went hand in hand in the struggle by which the Electors triumphed over local opposition. Interesting sidelights on Brandenburg-Prussia from the Roman Catholic point of view are to be found scattered through J. Janssen, *History of the German People at the Close of the Middle Ages* (17 vols., London, 1896–1925). F. L. Carsten, *The Origins of Prussia* (Oxford, 1954), by a German emigré historian living in England, is refreshing in its new perspective and freedom from age-old Prussian clichés. H. Holborn, *A History of Modern Germany* (2 vols., New York, 1959–1963) [with concluding volume still to come] is excellent in setting Prussian developments in their general German framework. The most recent textbook treatment is John E. Rodes, *Germany: A History* (New York, 1964).

The political and social organization of the Brandenburg household and administration in the later Middle Ages is given in detail in H. Spangenberg, *Hof und Zentralverwaltung der Mark Brandenburg im Mittelalter* (Leipzig, 1908), and in G. Schapper, *Die Hofordnung von 1470* (Leipzig, 1912). On the reception of the Roman law, see S. B. Fay, "The Roman Law and the German Peasant," in *American Hist. Review,* XVI, 241–254, January 1911.

The organization of the Estates in the sixteenth century is admirably described by M. Hass, *Die kurmärkischen Stände* (Leipzig, 1913); and the proceedings and debates of the Estates in their struggle with Joachim II, throwing a great deal of light on social, economic, and religious as well as constitutional and financial matters, are printed by W. Friedensburg, *Kurmärkische Ständeakten* (2 vols., Leipzig, 1913–1916). The standard account of the Teutonic Order is the classic study by H. von Treitschke *Origins of Prussianism* (London, 1942), originally published in 1862.

CHAPTER 2

The standard biography of the Great Elector is by M. Philippson, *Der Grosse Kurfürst Friedrich Wilhelm von Brandenburg* (3 vols., Berlin, 1897–1903). For good shorter accounts, see the illustrated biography by E. Heyck, *Der Grosse Kurfürst* (Bielefeld and Leipzig, 1902), and the popular work by F. Schevill, *The Great Elector* (Chicago, 1947). The most recent general account is by F. L. Carsten, "The Rise of Brandenburg," in *The New Cambridge Modern History*, Vol. V (Cambridge, 1961) pp. 543–558.

The social and economic conditions in Brandenburg at the close of the Thirty Years' War are summed up in the introduction to the Privy Council Records edited by O. Meinardus, *Protokolle und Relationen des Brandenburgischen Geheimen Rates* (7 vols., Berlin, 1889 ff.); these documents, which have been published for the years 1640 to 1667, are a mine of interesting information for every aspect of the Great Elector's internal administration.

His struggle with the Estates to establish his absolutism can be followed in detail in the other chief documentary publication for his reign: *Urkunden und Aktenstücke zur Geschichte des Kurfürsten Friedrich Wilhelm von Brandenburg* (23 vols., Berlin, 1864 ff.); Volumes 5, 10, and 15–16 deal respectively with Brandenburg, Cleves-Mark, and East Prussia). The opposition of Roth and Kalckstein is interestingly recounted by O. Nugel, "Der Schöppenmeister Hieronymous Roth" in *Forschungen zur Brandenburgischen und Preussischen Geschichte*, XIV, 393–479, 1901; by J. Paczkowski, "Der Grosse Kurfürst und Christian Ludwig von Kalckstein," *ibid.*, II, 407–513; III, 272–280, 419–463, 1889–1890; and by F. Hirsch, "Zur Geschichte Christian Ludwigs von Kalckstein," *ibid.*, III, 248–271, V, 299–310. A long needed statement of the case for the *Stände* (not, however, concentrating upon Prussia) can be found in F. L. Garsten, *Princes and Parliaments in Germany from the Fifteenth to the Eighteenth Century* (Oxford, 1959).

As to the Great Elector's foreign policy, there are good accounts of his part in the First Northern War by E. Haumant, *La Guerre du Nord* (Paris, 1893); of his shifting alliances after 1660 by G. Pages, *Le Grand Electeur et Louis XIV, 1660–1688* (Paris, 1905); and of his whole reign by A. Waddington, *Le Grand Electeur Frederic Guillaume de Brandenbourg: sa Politique Exterieur, 1640–1688* (2 vols., Paris, 1905–1908).

CHAPTER 3

For the history of Prussian administration in the eighteenth century, the *Acta Borussica* are fundamental. They comprise several series. (1) *Die Behördenorganisation* (ed. by G. Schmoller, O. Hintze, *et al.*, 15 vols., Berlin, 1894 ff., covering the years 1713 to 1772); this contains the documents, richly sprinkled with the pungent *marginalia* of Frederick William I and Frederick II, illustrating the development of the boards of government and the work of the General Directory. (2) *Getreidehandelspolitik* (ed. by G. Schmoller, G. Naude, and A. Skalweit, 4 vols., 1896–1931) on the government's policy of restricting the importation and exportation of grain, and of buying it up and storing it in plentiful years when the price was low. (3) *Münzwesen* (ed. by F. Freiherr von Schrötter, 6 vols., Berlin, 1904–1911) on the coinage system. (4) *Seidenindustrie* (ed. by G. Schmoller and O. Hintze, 3 vols., Berlin, 1892) on the silk industry. (5) *Wollenindustrie* (ed. by C. Hinrichs, Berlin, 1933) on the woolen industry under Frederick William I. To these should be added a work on the Hohenzollern zeal for settling colonists and improving agriculture, by R. Stadelmann, *Preussens Könige in ihrer Tätigkeit für die Landeskultur* (4 vols., Leipzig, 1878–1887).

Good general accounts of Germany, including Prussia, may be found in Sir Richard Lodge, *Great Britain and Prussia in the Eighteenth Century* (Oxford, 1923); W. H. Bruford, *Germany in the Eighteenth Century* (Cambridge, England, 1935);

K. S. Pinson, *Pietism as a Factor in the Rise of German Nationalism* (New York, 1934); and K. Francke, *History of German Literature, or Social Forces in German Literature* (New York, 1897).

There are several important books on Frederick William I. The best is J. Klepper, **Der Vater** (Berlin, 1937), despite the fact that it is in the form of a novel rather than historical treatise; the most scholarly C. Hinrichs, *Friedrich Wilhelm I. König in Preussen. Jugend und Aufstieg* (Leipzig, 1941), the first volume of an incompleted biography; the most readable F. von Oppen Bronikowski, *Der Baumeister des preussischen Staates* (Jena, 1934). R. R. Ergang, *The Potsdam Führer: Frederick William I, Father of Prussian Militarism* (New York, 1941) is a serviceable English study despite its preposterous title.

Two studies deal with Frederick William's strained relations with his brilliant son: E. Lavisse, *Youth of Frederick the Great* (London, 1891), a long established classic by an eminent French historian, and E. Simon, *The Making of Frederick the Great* (Boston, 1964), a recent popular account. The development of Frederick's political ideas is traced brilliantly by A. Berney, *Friedrich der Grosse. Entwicklungsgeschichte eines Staatsmannes* (Tübingen, 1934). Frederick's able brother Henry is covered definitively in the well-written biography by Chester Easum, *Prince Henry of Prussia, Brother of Frederick the Great* (Madison, 1942).

The standard biography of Frederick the Great is by the man who was long director of the Prussian archives, R. Koser, *König Friedrich der Grosse* (4 vols., Stuttgart, 1912). Thomas Carlyle's *Frederick the Great* (6 vols., London, 1858–1865) is a masterpiece of English literature, good for Frederick's campaigns and battles, very inadequate on diplomatic, institutional, and social history, and *sui generis* in style. The most interesting recent one-volume biography in German is G. Ritter, *Friedrich der Grosse: ein historisches Profil* (Leipzig, 1936), stimulating for its scholarship and for the parallels and lessons that it draws for Nazi Germany. A good introduction in English is G. P.

Gooch, *Frederick the Great. The Ruler, the Writer, the Man* (New York, 1947).

The best sources for the study of Frederick the Great in addition to the *Acta Borussica* mentioned above are his own voluminous writings, especially his *Politische Korrespondenz* (ed. by R. Koser, G. B. Volz, *et al.*, 46 vols., Berlin, 1879 ff.) comprising diplomatic, military, and miscellaneous dispatches, sometimes in German and sometimes in French, and covering, as far as published, the period 1740–1782; and the *Oeuvres de Frederic le Grand* (ed., by J. D. E. Preuss, 33 vols., Berlin, 1846–1857) comprising his literary writings: poems; correspondence with Voltaire, D'Argens, and other *philosophes;* histories of his ancestors, of his own times, and of the art of war; his attack on German literature; and a variety of other matters. The relationship between Frederick's statecraft and generalship is covered in the magisterial work of G. Ritter, *Staatskunst und Kriegshandwerk. Das Problem des "Militarismus" in Deutschland* (Vol. I, Munich, 1954). The much controverted problem of the origins of the Seven Years' War has been recently reexamined by H. Butterfield: "The Reconstruction of an Historical Episode: The History of the Enquiry into the Origins of the Seven Years' War," *Man on His Past* (Boston, 1960), pp. 143–170. Manfred Schlenke, *England und das friderizianische Preussen 1740–1763* (Freiburg, 1963) is a pioneering study on how Frederick appeared to contemporary English public opinion.

On the First Partition of Poland, see A. Sorel, *The Eastern Question in the Eighteenth Century* (London, 1898) for the European setting; R. H. Lord, *The Second Partition of Poland* (Cambridge, Mass., 1915, Introduction) for the weaknesses of Poland; the recent study by Herbert Kaplan, *The First Partition of Poland* (New York, 1962), asserting that Austria was the main culprit; and for Frederick the Great's share in the partition, two articles by G. B. Volz in *Forschungen zur Brandb. Preuss. Geschichte* 18:151–201 and 23:71–143, 224–225, and M.

Bär, *Westpreussen unter Friedrich dem Grossen* (2 vols., Leipzig, 1909).

Harold Temperley, *Frederic the Great and Kaiser Joseph* (London, 1915), and Leopold von Ranke, *Die deutschen Mächte und der Furstenbund* (Leipzig, 1875) give excellent accounts of Frederick II's efforts to hold in leash his restless Austrian neighbor.

Frederick's methods of work as an enlightened despot are very interestingly described in the penetrating study of W. L. Dorn, "The Prussian Bureaucracy in the Eighteenth Century" in the *Political Science Quarterly,* 46: 403–423; 47: 75–94, 259–273 (September, 1931–June, 1932). Frederick's judicial reforms are examined in the useful monograph of H. Weill, *Frederick the Great and Samuel von Cocceji* (Madison, 1961). The best book on the Prussian law codification (which was completed only after Frederick's death but bears the imprint of his age) is Uwe-Jens Heuer, *Allgemeines Landrecht und Klassenkampf. Die Auseinandersetzung um die Prinzipien des Allgemeinen Landrechts* (East Berlin, 1960) despite its use of much Marxist jargon; a good brief introduction is H. Conrad, *Die Geistigen Grundlagen des Allgemeinen Landrechts* (Cologne, 1958). A pioneering monograph on the condition of the Junker nobility is F. Martiny, *Die Adelsfrage in Preussen vor 1806 als politisches und soziales Problem* (Stuttgart, 1938). Hans Rosenberg, *Bureaucracy, Aristocracy and Autocracy: The Prussian Experience 1660–1815* (Cambridge, Mass, 1958) is an important work of administrative and social history that stresses the seamy side of Prussian affairs.

Index